REFLECTIONS IN RHYME

REFLECTIONS IN RHYME

by

BERTHA KLUG

Made and printed by
REGENCY PRESS (London and New York) LTD.
125 HIGH HOLBORN, LONDON WC1V 6QA

CONTENTS

Page

"Dedicated to my husband who prevailed upon me to compile my verses into a book."

THINK ON THESE THINGS

Written mainly for my children,
    That they may bear in mind,
While life presents its many problems
    It also—they will find,
Brings many joys and blessings
    So often gone unseen,
Lost in regret and self pity
    Of "Things that might have been"

But also that they should remember
    That when things have gone awry,
To learn a lesson from it
    Not just sit down and cry,
Or to pretend it never happened
    That could drive one quite insane,
No "Pick yourself up, Brush yourself down
    And start all over again"

Reflections in Rhyme

Part One :

ON AWARENESS AND RELATIONSHIPS

AWARENESS

Five senses we've been given
    and we take them so for granted
Tending to ignore, that we'd enjoy them more
If we would use them,
    as they were intended.

Look for beauty with the eyes,
    Then life would seem less troubled,
It would take the frown, turn it upside down,
Bringing contentment; and blessings
    would emerge—doubled.

Listen to music, or the sweet sound of nature
    To give the ears relief
From incessant noise, or a grating voice
That's discontented, or bent
    On stirring up mischief.

Our tongues were given specially
    to help us to communicate;
For each other to reach, with the power of speech,
But with love and kindness,
    Not bitterness and hate.

We've polluted our atmosphere,
    and produced smells that offend,
But flowers and trees, give forth scents that please.
So to mother nature go, fill lungs and nostrils
    As God did surely intend.

5

Our food being mainly produced
    by aids that are artificial,
It's a terrible waste, but we've lost the taste
For the earth's natural foods,
    which are more beneficial.

These are our five senses,
    but the greatest sense to possess,
Is used so rare, namely being aware.
For to develop wisely the senses,
    above all what one needs—is awareness.

GIVING IS LIVING

Give a thought when'er you can
    To those in need around you
Give a smile to whom you meet,
    And feel its warmth abound you too.

Give a word of kindness
    To those you speak to daily,
Give an ear to someone's troubles
    And listen to them—carefully.

Give a little of your time
    To others who are lonely,
Give some money—if it's needed,
    But not just money only.

Give your eyes to things around you
    Make yourself aware,
Give them room within your mind
    To enjoy them, and to care.

Give a prayer of thankfulness
    For things you've been receiving,
Feel contentment in the knowledge
    That giving is living—
        And loving is giving.

BARRIERS

We struggle hard to break the barriers
   Of gravity, time and sound,
Searching for things high above us
   Neglecting those near and around.

Those dreadful barriers that we know
   Of race, colour, and creed,
Causing intolerance and hatred
   And cruelty in man do breed.

Then there's the barrier of language
   Keeping men far apart,
Preventing communication—
   Let us break that for a start.

And the barriers of boundaries
   Won usually by fighting wars,
Driving people here and there
   All in the name of "the cause".

If suddenly there appeared
   From somewhere out in space
An enemy bent on destroying us all,
   It would unite the human race.

For eventually man will conquer
   Every barrier there is up above,
How much better to do it here
   With understanding, kindness and love.

THE THREE DISGRACES
FEAR, HATRED AND COWARDICE

Man is baffled and bewildered
  By the things he does not know,
Wondering the effect it will have on him
  Whether he should stay or go,
What will tomorrow bring him
  Should he say yes or no;
Fear of the unknown—man's tormentor
  And just fearing fear—keeping him low.

And from fear stems hatred
  Such a common and fatal disease,
Developing in man agressions
  Never leaving him in peace,
And hatred then breeds hatred
  So it's ever on the increase;
Hatred—a distorted evil emotion
  And where it exists—there's no peace.

And how do we view cowardice
  Maybe the worst disgrace of all,
Preventing man from preventing evil
  And allowing it to take its toll;
So to eradicate the three disgraces
  On all our good senses we need to call,
Including those oft forgotten three graces
  Faith, Hope and Charity—cleansers of the Soul.

FRIENDSHIP

Friendship is a most precious thing,
A relationship one should treasure,
But a real friend is one who is there
To share your sorrows as well as pleasure.

It's not a proof of friendship
To sit and gossip every day
On the telephone, or meet for lunch
To criticise what others do or say.

A really true friend is someone
On who's support you can always rely,
With whom you can pick up the threads,
No matter how much time has gone by.

And with friends who live far away
Even those across the seas,
It's good to try and keep in touch,
A nicely worded letter will always please.

For isn't it a lovely feeling
When the postman has a letter for you,
But you must give to receive
So remember, you must write too.

But above all to keep a friend,
Just remember the following phrase,
Do not listen to idle gossip,
"Judge no man till you stand in his place".

TO FORGIVE

When things are going wrong
for you
Through no fault of your
own,
When injustice is hurled at
you
And you feel bewildered
and alone,
When the very good you do
Is thrown back in your
face,
When you find you're trapped
Unable to take the pace,
When you turn to friends
for help
And find that they don't
care
Even though when they
had troubles
You were always there,
Don't feel hurt and bitter
And let hatred in your
heart
Don't try to seek vengeance
It will only tear you apart.
Do what you can to put
things right
Leave no stone unturned,
Then say, you're that much
wiser
Through the heartache you
have learned
That we can't always
choose
What happens while we live
We might not be able to
forget
But we must learn to
forgive.

COMMUNICATION

Striving to reach across the miles
   Every year brings a new invention
To get nearer, quicker and clearer,
   But what is man's intention?
Nearer in order to hurt and destroy
   Or to understand each other more?
The obstacle is not in the miles
   But in the communication we ignore.

Have you ever felt lonely in a crowd
   Though intensely chatting away,
Wishing you were somewhere else
   Where talking meant something to say?
For the word is the messenger
   From one's lips to another ear,
Often on its journey, becoming distorted,
   Its message no longer clear.

When aiming to communicate
   We need the right words to use,
Or else the words received
   Are muddled and confuse.
To convey a scene, a joy, pain or sorrow
   Requires words, that are suitable,
Yet so often are we lost
   In the confusion of a Tower of Babel.

The aeroplane brings us nearer faster
   The silver screen takes us to the spot,
The telephone and radio are instant links,
   But in the sum total, what have we got?
Surely man's salvation lies this way,
   In true communication—Oh if only we could
For so much is said,
   And so little understood.

11

LOYALTY

Love—you claim
    you have for me,
        but what is love
            without loyalty.

Or do the unkind glances
    escape free,
        and are you deaf to the comments
            that hurt deeply.

YET when the target is yourself,
    one cannot help but see
        how quickly you protest,
            and vehemently.

Awareness of each other's feelings,
    do you not agree,
        promotes understanding,
            the need for loyalty.

Loyalty though stands not alone,
    but in turn has to be,
        tempered with discretion,
            and judged accurately.

There being those situations
    one cannot always foresee,
        when Solomon's wisdom is needed
            to decide justly.

Your loyalty may at times be divided,
    and the decisions will not come easy.
        For so often, being loyal to one
            will spell for another—disloyalty.

THEY KNOW ME NOT

They've travelled with me
      through most of my life,
They've judged me—mostly wrongly.
For seeing things
      with unseeing eyes,
means seeing things unfeelingly.

How would they know
      of my heartaches,
Of injustices and hurts galore,
How could they know
      that behind that smile,
Beat a heart in a body
      wearied and sore,
Clutching at straws of happiness
      that lingered for a while.

How could they see
      beneath the clothes
   and adornments, ornate and masking
The feelings of an imprisoned soul,
      and—for want of those things
That would let it breathe—dying.

And such simple wants
      that would help it live.
Like time to listen, to walk in the woods,
      to discard pretence
         to be free of chains,
To supply the needy—and to give.

What know you of me
      that think you know me a lot,
You know nothing
      or my unseen scars—
Think again if you will,
      For, for sure, you know me not.

13

UNDERSTANDING

When I close my eyes at night
I ask the Lord above,
Please give me understanding
To help the ones I love.

For joy, peace, happiness
We should aim to bring
To family, friends, to everyone
And for this we need—understanding.

Understanding the many problems
Which daily one has to face,
The ability to deal with them
And in their proper place.

To understand you have to see
Not only with your eyes,
And words often confuse
No matter how one tries.

Listen, and look at the facts
That are being told to you,
Put yourself in the place
Of the teller's point of view.

So when we close our eyes at night
Let us ask the Lord above,
To help us understand understanding,
To help the ones we love.

A LETTER TO THE COMMUNITY—WELFARE?

What are we, that in the twilight of our lives
We have to be burdens—struggling to survive.

Our

Experiences of a lifetime, constantly come crowding in,
Explain so much we could, but where would we begin.

For

Living for us, has been a long endurance test,
Looks like we've failed, though we've tried to do our best.

Good

Fortune having eluded us, we're in need of financial aid,
For us though, the loneliness is the hardest—like buried before
dead.

We're

Asking so little, for really our needs are few,
And if we're an insoluble problem, we apologise to you.

Now

Relying on the young, the strong, the wise, the kind,
Really is all we can do, before leaving this world behind.

But

Even though on you good people we need to rely,
Ever remember the phrase, "But for the grace of God there go I."

THE MESSAGE OF FREEMASONRY

The gathering of the members
The hum from the chattering,
The call to order—Silence,
And open once more—The meeting.

The precision and the dignity
Is lovely to behold
The beginners, the learned ones
The mixture of young and old.

All there for a purpose
To improve, and open the mind
To show mercy and charity
To men of every kind.

The words—So meaningful
Whether spoken or read,
Oh! If only man meant
the things that he said.

For it's easy to pay lip service
And not bother about the deed
But a true Mason would feel compelled
To help a brother in need.

When one's been blessed with plenty
And of problems had very few
'Tis hard to remember, though it's 'others' today
That tomorrow, it could be you.

For we all came equal in the world;
And remember always, we must,
That we leave just as equal
Ashes to ashes, and dust to dust.

Listening to the ritual, one feels
Somehow, "Nearer my God to thee"
Absorbing the words of wisdom
Through the medium of freemasonry.

PERSON-AL-ITY

In the hustle and bustle of living
   There is very little time to think.
The babe is born, the adult emerges,
   Old age approaches, life is over in a wink.

But, to every person that is born,
   A personal personality is presented,
That will with understanding love,
   Develop, as nature really intended.

So often a personality is sadly crushed
   By well intentioned, but wrong advice
With emphasis that, it's nice to be important,
   Whereas, it's more important to be nice.

But then as older grows the child
   Parents should loosen the reins
For the true personality evolves from experience,
   From personal successes, difficulties and pains.

To enable children to know themselves
   One must allow them plenty of scope,
And the best way to provide protection,
   Is by equipping them with the ability to cope.

But to finally discover who and what we are,
   We ourselves must provide the key,
By looking outward to nature, and into oneself.
   Each one will find his own person-al-ity.

Part Two :

ON LOVE AND MARRIAGE

WHAT IS A CHILD—A WIFE—A MOTHER?

Throughout my childhood memories
Whether things went right or wrong,
There was never depression in our home
And always time for a song.

With this example before me,
I learned what it is to cope
With whatever suddenly confronted me
Never to despair—Always to hope!

And so when it came to marriage
And difficulties did arise,
I knew that trouble must be dealt with
No matter what its size.

Always you must balance the scales
For life is made that way,
One day can be up—and one day down,
But you must live it day by day.

And when the children start to come
And thank God they did to us,
Each problem must be dealt with,
If possible, with a minimum of fuss.

And so, on looking back,
This lesson I know I've learned,
You must be able to divide yourself
And judge with what to be concerned.

Is it as the child when
Things go wrong with Dad or Mum?
Or is it as the wife, to know when to speak
And when to appear dumb?

Or is it as the Mother
As each stage children go through,
And they have problems to cope with
And need advice and help from you?

Sometimes you feel like an 'in-between'
And don't know which course to take,
But if your heart and head are firm
The correct decision you'll make.

But in order to succeed in this,
You must pray to have good health,
For with this, you are equipped for anything
Its blessings are far more than wealth.

THE FAMILY

The world has known
    Since time began,
That man needs woman
    And woman needs man.

And so in a Family
    Both parents have their Role,
Without either one—
    The Family is not whole.

But truly it's not enough
    Just being there,
Contribute, take interest
    Show how much you care.

19

To ensure a happy Family
　To see the jobs well done,
Both should co-operate
　It's just too much for one.

For as in a healthy body
　All organs we need,
The same applies in a Family
　For it to function and succeed.

Both Parents have a place
　Each must play a part
The man is the head
　The woman, the heart.

THE TALE OF TWO TERRYS or WHAT IS MARRIAGE?

Terry Jay lived in a big house
Where servants they did employ,
With lots of money and beautiful clothes,
And yet he was a sad little boy.

For Terry's parents had parted,
Daddy had gone away
And Mummy was always busy,
When Terry asked her to play.

He would sit by his bedroom window
And gaze into the street,
And picture in his little mind
A really wonderful treat.

He was at the Zoo with Dad and Mum
Or maybe just out for a ride,
Or packing for the summer holidays
To go to their favourite seaside.

And then suddenly he'd remember
That this could never be,
For soon there was to be a divorce,
They were no longer a family.

There lived another Terry
At the other end of town,
In a small and shabby cottage
On which the rich would frown.

And Terry's clothes were old
They'd been worn by Tim his brother,
And sometimes there wasn't much to eat
Which distressed Terry's Dad and Mother.

But Terry Brown was a happy boy
And enjoyed each and every day,
For love lived in that home,
It might be shabby, but it was always gay.

For if ever he had problems,
And of course, all children do,
He knew there was always someone
He could take his troubles to.

A trouble shared is a trouble halved
Then things don't look so bad,
And Terry always felt secure
In the love of his Mum and Dad.

This story of course, has a moral
Which is that it's love that brings
Happiness, security and peace of mind,
Far more than material things.

But how often does it happen
That marriages go off course,
And despite there being children
They end up in divorce.

How can something which starts so right
Go so completely wrong,
Or is it because they haven't worked
To make their marriage strong?

For make no mistake about it,
Even if in heaven the marriage is made,
A successful marriage means hard work
If you don't want the love to fade.

Just think of the amount of effort
That's given in all walks of life,
Business, professions and hobbies,
Yet often so little between man and wife.

If a husband returns from work
Obviously weary and tired,
An understanding, sympathetic wife
Is the one to be admired.

And a husband should always remember
That a wife likes to feel wanted,
She too works hard, and without pay,
So don't take her too much for granted.

Of course, a successful marriage
Does not earn money or any other award,
But a happy, secure and stable home
Brings its own priceless reward.

THE WEDDING

Slowly walking down the aisle,
The scent of flowers in the air,
The organ playing, the choir singing,
Brings a thrill beyond compare.

The beauty of the wedding service
Delivered with much dignity;
The pleasure of a well-spoken sermon,
The blessings sung with such sincerity.

Then the greatest moment of all,
The glass is smashed, "Mazeltov" we say;
Kisses all round, just a few tears,
But mainly all is happy and gay.

Then on to the wedding feast,
The guests are greeted one by one,
All so beautifully attired
And all ready for the fun.

We then sit down to dinner,
And get up fit to burst,
Wine and champagne flowing;
No one can complain of thirst.

The usual run of toasts,
Everyone praised sky high,
Then dancing, "Auld Lang Syne", "The Queen",
My, how the time does fly.

The reluctant good night kisses,
Much praise—for all was perfection;
And then the sad realization,
That life is anticipation and reflection.

For after months of planning
We now speak of what has been,
The actual episode itself
Is gone, in a flash, like a dream.

And that is how life is,
Memories all the way,
So let us make them good ones,
And keep the bad ones at bay.

And to the young couple,
Whose new life starts in Shul;
Try to cling to precious moments,
Enjoy them to the full.

WRITTEN FOR OUR SILVER WEDDING

We don't want to bore you with speeches
We want you to relax and be gay
But we can't help reminiscing a little
On this—our Silver Wedding Day.
A lot of things can happen—and did—
In the span of twenty-five years;
They've brought us pleasure and laughter.
And more than our share of tears.
But no matter what the crises
And of those we have quite a lot
We always remembered grandma's words
"Oh God, frighten me, but punish me not."
For nowhere has it been written
That as we journey through our life
The path is smoothed before us
And free from trouble and strife
So we've tried to balance the scales
By counting our blessings each day,
And to those in the early stage of marriage
There's a small message we'd like to convey
For a successful, happy marriage,
In which the couple remain enchanted,
Take each other for better or worse,
But never, never for granted,
We're grateful to the Almighty
For the blessings that he sends;
We're happy to have here with us
Our very dear family and friends,
We miss those who were with us
Today, twenty-five years ago
But we think of them constantly
And feel sure that they know.
And now our fervent wishes are
That please God as we journey further,
You will all be blessed with good health,
Happiness and peace. With love. Isy and Bertha.

A STRING OF PEARLS

Written for our Pearl Wedding

To compensate for life's numerous problems,
  We need to seek and create our own fun,
So it's good to have family gatherings,
  And any excuse is better than none.
But in fact today we have several;
  So I'll begin now with number one.

It's much joy to our dear Essie and Eddie,
  And of course Howard and Michael too,
On the marriage next month in Israel
  Of Ruthi to Barry—son number two,
And while he's skipped the queue a bit,
  We all agree it is the right thing to do.

Good luck as well to the Grandparents,
  Who are unable the journey to make,
You three we had in mind also,
  So this evening is partly for your sake.
And as the same applies to most of our guests,
  With us—all your good wishes we'll take.

Which leads me into another excuse,
  And that is, that tomorrow we leave
On our journey to Israel for the wedding,
  Something which I can hardly believe,
For after the experience of the past two years,
  It's for me personally—a kind of reprieve.

There's one further reason why we're all here today,
  Partaking of this humble feast,
And it's our gratitude and thankfulness,
  Therefore we could not resist,
A small remembrance of this anniversary,
  So while it's last—it's not least on the list.

25

And now forgive me a moment's nostalgia,
   But it does include many who are present.
For while we're occupied with daily living,
   And involved with 'episodes' as they're sent
It's only now, thirty years later, that we observe,
   How swiftly those thirty years went.

Does it not seem—like only yesterday,
   Petherton Road, the Waltzers, the Pinkerfeld girls?
The years have left a trail of memories,
   And as each one of them unfurls,
We've collected them, and strung them together,
   And made of them a String of Pearls.

ODE TO BARRY AND RUTHI

Give me a man with courage
        determination and grit,

Add the ingredients of sympathy,
        understanding and wit,

Put them together and they spell success
        one surely must admit,

And who else but Barry Bluston
        does this description fit?

But then we must not forget
        one other excellent quality,

It's his good taste—like choosing for wife
        sweet, petite pretty Ruthi,

Who endeared herself to us all on sight
        for she's loved by all our family,

For her charm, wisdom, clarity of mind
        and obvious love for Barry.

When two such characters in marriage are joined
    as you two now have done,

You have the basis for perfect harmony
    if to each other you remain number one.

Sharing always life's varied experiences
    good or bad as they come,

So our wishes are for your good health always
    to crowd your blessed union.

Part Three :

THOUGHTS FROM A SICK BED

While lying here I remember
And recall so vividly,
Countless and various incidents
That live in my memory.

Times when there was plenty
And times when things were bad,
Mostly there was laughter,
But sometimes we were sad.

As when a loved one left us,
Or war reared its ugly head,
All these things I remember
As I lie here in my bed.

The time when I was married,
Or when the children came.
If I lived my life over
I'd want it all the same.

The times when the children were naughty
And the times when they were good,
Their illnesses or successes,
These are the joys of motherhood.

I think of the many interests
I've had and thoroughly enjoyed,
Music, Theatre, Poetry, Needlework,
How better can one be employed?

And now my only wish is,
And I pray for it fervently,
Dear God, make me better soon,
Please return my health to me.

THE PATIENT'S DILEMMA

Science has advanced so rapidly,
Greater than the mind can conceive,
And we see and hear of wonders
In which we can hardly believe

We aim to reach the ocean's depths
Or fly up to outer space,
But aren't we neglecting earthly things
And ignoring the human race?

Is the medical profession
Really doing the best it can
To alleviate the sufferings
That frequently beset man?

We know that doctors are not infallible
And being human can make a mistake
God will provide the miracles,
But how much can a patient take?

There is an attitude of casualness,
Nature's symptoms are ignored,
Even the guide of a temperature
Doesn't seem to strike a chord

And for the patient who strongly feels
That something is definitely wrong,
He has to hold on till the cause is found
Hold on and pray, no matter how long.

But for some this is impossible
And they fall by the way
Because of some small medical error,
They have seen their last day.

In any other trade or profession
When mistakes or troubles occur,
One queries and questions
For it is human to err.

But not to doctors and nurses,
They've raised themselves so high,
That no matter what wrong they do
You are not permitted to ask why.

And then to add insult to injury
You're promptly presented with the bill,
They conveniently ignore the fact
That you are probably still ill.

So let's come back to earth again
And think of those who live today,
Instead of devoting so much time
To the wonders and glories far away.

TRANQUILITY

To waken with the birds, feeling tranquil,
Having slept through the night with ease,
Without the aid of the eternal pill,
Means starting the day in harmony and peace.

But how to reach this Utopia you ask,
When the mind's in constant confusion?
While it can be done, it's no easy task,
Of this, let us have no illusion.

Firstly, we must learn how to begin
To understand our thoughts and mind,
Making sure we are able to look within,
And not to our own faults be blind.

Do we expect too much of ourselves,
Or, more often than not, of others—
Is it injustices tucked away on shelves
Done to us—or from us, to our brothers.

Whichever it is, it was done in the past
And forever that time has gone,
So dwelling upon it, only makes it last,
And cannot change what is done.

So now we'll look to the future instead.
Let us start by making new vows,
And a good time to do it, is at night in bed
It's the one thing, that sleeplessness allows.

Vow to forgive those who have wronged you,
It's unhappy thoughts that keep one awake.
For the wrong you have done, forgive yourself too,
Vowing never the same mistake to make.

And now a few thoughts you must spare
For those who view your life with envy,
Who think of you as free from care,
Oh yes my friend—this will ever be.

Vow now to discard depression for belief,
To cast out the enemy, self pity
Which cloaks the blessings buried beneath,
And robs us of sleep and tranquility.

HOW TO VISIT A PATIENT

We've rules on how to dress
  Rules on etiquette
Rules on keeping youthful
  Slim and fit—and yet
Although we've rules for beauty
  And other rules galore,
We've missed out on one rule
  Of "How to be a Visitor".

"How to be a Visitor?"
  I can almost hear you say
"What does one need to know

31

Just the hour and the day,
The patient's taste in chocolates,
    Fruit, the books they read,
The flowers they like
    What else does a patient need?"

What a patient needs from a visitor
    Is someone who is kind,
Sympathetic, understanding,
    And also doesn't mind
Listening to the patient
    Who spends many hours awake
In pain, discomfort, apprehension
    So don't make the mistake

Made by so many
    Probably in innocence
Lack of knowledge—or
    Just plain cold ignorance.
To be a good visitor
    Requires just the right touch,
Don't stay too long
    Or talk too much.

Don't burden the patient
    With many tales of woe
Don't swell the numbers
    If there's too many visitors—go,
Two at a time is quite enough
    For often after that,
The visitors forget the patient
    And to each other chat.

If you're of a nervous nature
    And with a certain fear
Of hospitals and illnesses
    And so unable to hear
The sort of thing a patient
    Sometimes has to endure,
Then keep away, your visit
    Will not help the cure.

Do you go to see a patient
    For their sake—or is it
That you feel you ought to?
    Don't—if it's just a duty visit.
It would be kinder, more thoughtful
    And altogether better
To send a card, some flowers
    Or a nicely worded letter.

But a patient does need visitors
    And looks forward to them too,
So it's most important for visitors
    To know what to do.
Apart from the rules, visitors
    Should use their common sense,
Remember when visiting, do it calmly
    Kindly, and always with patience.

MEMORIES

Written for my children, Harold, Anthony, Brian and Francesca
in the "New England" hospital, Boston, Mass., U.S.A.

As I lie here so lonely;
Passing through my mind
Are memories, thoughts and faces
All of a different kind.

Memories of my childhood,
Of fun and laughter gay,
The many ups and downs of life
As I've journeyed on my way.

Faces of the dear departed,
Whose memories still remain.
What I'd give if only
I could see them once again.

33

But uppermost in my mind,
As I recall these memories,
Are the faces of the loved ones
I've left across the seas.

Of our normal life together
Before this year of trial.
Of my pleasurable duties
I enjoyed without denial

I close my eyes and picture
Us six around the table
And pray it won't be long now
Before I will be able

To rejoin my lovely family
Three sons and a daughter who
Though individuals and different
Are solidly united too.

I think of my first-born Harold,
Of his calm and gentle ways,
His wise and steady judgment
Commands the highest praise.

And then of mischievious Anthony,
Who is always full of fun,
But also keeps a level head,
I'm proud of you, my son.

With pure pleasure I think of Brian
And his talents of various sorts,
Playing and writing, music and poetry,
Yet gifted in the field of sports.

And my sweet darling Francesca
With her happy smiling face,
Whether swimming, playing or "helping"
No one can take her place

Being always with them,
Picking them up when they fell
Metaphorically and physically,
I feel I know them well.

And now I'd like the chance
To be able to enjoy once more
Their company, and other things
Just as I did before.

THE MENACE IN MEDICINE

Doctor, dear doctor, this is a cry from the heart!
But how do I reach you, my message to impart?

What I have to tell you, I've experienced not contrived,
It's what I've witnessed and endured—and yet survived.

You spend years in training, and there's much that you learn,
But you lose the human touch—and that is my concern.

You've forgotten how to listen, which can lead to complication,
Confident you can call upon, newly invented medication.

And that's a modern menace! instant reliance on drugs,
Interfering with nature and blaming it on the 'bugs'.

You take the Hippocratic oath—which if I'm not mistaken,
Dedicates you to your patient—an oath often sadly forsaken.

For truly it's hypocritical, when your profession is abused,
By ignoring nature's symptoms, and your patient becomes confused;

Or confused with another patient—yet you feel so sure,
And you back your opinion, and arrogantly prescribe the 'cure'.

For how glibly you give an opinion, and call it a diagnosis,
And should the condition not respond, it's then labelled 'neurosis'.

So, what you're missing and needing—and to me it's very plain,
Is one year for a course, to learn to be human again.

To help rid you of "The I, the me, myself"
Oh physician, physician be wise, and heal thyself.

THE RETURN VIA NATURE CURE

When the road's been hard and lonely and
paved with suffering and pain, your whole being
in disharmony, in a way that's hard to explain;
you feel it's been a worthwhile journey when
you're back among the living once again.

Having experienced one of life's tests, having fallen,
and then been revived, makes clear, that we're here,
only as God's guests, with much that can be derived;
If only we'd realise how much we've been blessed, when
mercifully we've survived.

It's on such a journey as this that I have been,
and just returned; Mundane daily tasks to me are
bliss, and there's much that I have learned, for
when my health went awry, amiss, and I was daily tossed
and turned, fervently for help to come did I
pray, and slowly but surely it did; and very simply—
via nature's way, through toxic poisons being rid!
Maybe all men will heed nature one day, and do as
she does bid.

It's then we'll reduce the doctors' bills, and
aids that are artificial, discarding all kinds
of drugs and pills, whose cures are merely superficial;
and learn that it's correct eating that prevents most
of our ills, that nature's way is harmonious, and
therefore beneficial.

THE DOCTOR SIMPLY SAYS

Put your hand in the bottle, and take out a pill
    The Doctor simply says
It should make you better, but it could make you ill,
    never mind—the Doctor simply says.

Put your trust in me and question me not,
    The Doctor simply says,
If I experiment enough, I'll find out what you've got,
    don't worry—the Doctor simply says.

You'd best come into hospital, be under our care
    The Doctor simply says
We'll inject you here, and inject you there,
    You'll be O.K.—The Doctor simply says.

Now we'll need some X-rays, and a variety of tests
    The Doctor simply says,
Nothing's revealed. Some patients really are pests,
    So glibly—the Doctor simply says.

Doubts creep in. But you're receiving the best attention
    The Doctor simply says.
Though the patient feels it's more like tension.
    You're wrong—the Doctor simply says.

I think we'd better open you up, take a look inside
    The Doctor simply says.
By now you're a rag no thought, no will, no pride,
    Knowing only—the Doctor simply says.

We've given you the works, we don't think it's physical
    The Doctor simply says,
Must be in your mind, purely psychological
    With finality—The Doctor simply says.

Part Four :

ON GOD AND NATURE

I GIVE THANKS

When I open my eyes in the morning
I give thanks and say,
Be there sun or rain outside,
Thank you, for a lovely day.

For no matter what the weather
It makes no difference to me,
I just go about my duties
With thanks—and joyfully.

I hear the sweet birds singing
And I'm singing with them too
I rise early, am busy all day,
And I give thanks to You.

For many months I suffered
Discomfort, weariness, pains
I was alive but not living
My hands and feet were in chains.

But though the road was rough
Never once did I despair,
I knew You'd not desert me
That always You were there.

Now I walk along the shore
With strong and winged feet,
The sea lapping on the sand
The air is good and sweet.

I feel as if I'm born again
And work is fun for me,
Daily I count my blessings,
Humbly, I give thanks to Thee.

MY GARDEN AND ME or WHY I BELIEVE

I sit in my garden and listen
And sweet sounds come to please,
The twitter of birds, the crickets
The rustle of the leaves on the trees,
The flutter of butterfly wings
The busy buzzing of the bees.

I sit in my garden and gaze,
And there's much to please my eyes,
Primulas, azaleas, tulips
Rhododendrons, majestic in size
Bushes with the buds of roses,
Though cloaked now in disguise.

I sit in my garden and breathe
And life seems devoid of care,
The perfume of wallflowers and lilac
Comes wafting through the air,
The scent of the new mown lawn,
Such moments like these are rare.

I sit in my garden and touch
The leaf on the twig, the bark on the tree,
The velvet petals of the flowers
Like tissue in their delicacy,
The strong blades of grass
The shrubs, the beds, brown and earthy.

I sit in my garden while eating
And the food improves to the taste,
But I think of those who go hungry
And wonder why in our haste
We take for granted God's gifts to us,
Which so wilfully we waste.

39

I sit in my garden and I feel
The spirit of goodness around,
Revealing itself from the sky, through wind
    and clouds,
Through the abundant growth from the ground;
I know that it's there—from the touch,
The taste, the smell, the sight, the sound.

FOR THE LOVE OF GOD

Oh say, what is that thing called love?
    which very few enjoy.
Love—true love, not just that certain something
    known twixt girl and boy.
Love—for and to, all that around us is,
    —and not just of self,
But mistake not loving for having,
    for possession of wealth.
Or possessing those near and dear ones,
    for whom love you declare,
For loving is caring, not clinging,
    a desire to help and to share.
And it's not enough to talk of love, reveal it,
    make sure that it shows.
For giving love, begets love, and slowly but surely,
    —that's the way it grows.
It's to Man's love of possession,
    World conflicts we can trace,
In its wake bringing war, hunger, disease
    and escalating the arms race.
So please let's stop and turn about,
    Listen and learn from the psalms,
So that for the love of God, and World peace,
    We race, with love—into each other's arms.

THE POWER OF PRAYER

Trouble roams around the world,
Why, no-one can explain,
Leaving its trail of problems
Could be misfortune, sickness, pain
And we have to restore ourselves,
For we hide from it in vain.

It comes to all of us in time,
Sometime, somehow, somewhere,
A sorrow, loss or illness
Which seems too hard to bear,
It's then we should remember
The comfort and power of prayer.

For there isn't any doubt,
That when all else appears to fail,
When all aids known to man
Have been tried to no avail,
Prayer will give you back hope
And help to lift the veil.

THE BEAUTY OF NATURE

Is mankind—really so blind
    That it cannot see,
The beautiful things that surround us
    Put there for you and me.

Do we close our eyes—or fail to realise
    The beauty of a tree,
Naked in Winter—clothed in Summer
    And in Spring a delight to see.

The flap of wings—the bird that sings
    The lambs that frolic free,
The different colours that emerge
    From the land so wondrously.

To see the earth—giving birth
　To so much—so suddenly,
Showing us great promise
　Of things that soon will be.

To see on high—a clear blue sky
　Or a sunset in all its glory,
These things are real for us to enjoy
　Not something we read in a story.

The moon at night giving us light
　And so helping us to see,
Or the twinkling stars in the heavens
　Without all this, what would life be.

There is much more—nature has in store
　As she gives forth with her beauty
So let us benefit from God's good work
　Not just view it all—from duty.

HARMONY

Most of us desire and try to attain
　to live our lives peacefully,
So when weighed down with problems,
　query and protest, vehemently,
Absolving ourselves of course
　from any personal responsibility;
Or maybe we find consolation
　in resigned inevitability.
We should try to avoid those people,
　with whom one needs to step warily,
For fear of inducing criticism or friction,
　with voices raised angrily;
And where there is no understanding
　or a lack of sympathy,
For it could leave one resentful,
　or with a feeling of apathy,
And either emotion produces tensions
　that creep up insidiously,
Until one finds oneself bodily bruised,
　and with a crushed personality.

But this is the price we pay
    for failing to live harmoniously,
Yet the power lies within us,
    to produce calm and tranquility,
By reversing the procedure, and it's done
    with the utmost simplicity.
Just think of a beautiful garden
    that displays its growth abundantly,
Or a proud orchard of trees
    giving forth its produce yearly.
Recall the movement of melodious music,
    or dancing performed gracefully,
Hear the sweet sounds from children
    when laughing spontaneously;
And what of the joy of two minds,
    meeting simultaneously?
Twice is said with half the words
    when they're spoken unreservedly.
Then observe a flock of birds
    flapping their wings rhythmically,
For no matter the speed, they fly with ease
    and perfect regularity.
And when we can apply these examples of rhythm,
    into our own lives daily,
Then, just like when a pebble thrown into water,
    sends vibrations endlessly,
So we could cause a chain reaction
    of perpetual harmony.

WITH GRATITUDE

With a heart that's light I arise,
    With gratitude I view each day,
Thankful that now, I am able to help
    Other souls who have lost their way.

Oh what a test it was dear God,
    painful and so often lonely;
But I felt so sure, that help would come,
    And come from you Lord only.

With fervour, daily did I pray,
 every morning, noon and night,
Till eventually the path was clear,
 I opened my eyes and saw the light.

From the depths I have emerged,
 But with much that I have learned;
My health is now restored to me,
 Hard won, and truly earned.

Having experienced man's incompetence,
 and sadly his arrogant attitude,
Having survived, with your help, the consequence,
 I greet each day, with joy and gratitude.

I WILL

I will — treat each day as a lifetime
I will — greet it with joy in my heart,
I will — balance the scales of life's problems
I will — if hope fails, accept it in good part.

I will — avoid despair, or blaming my luck,
I will — take good care not to repeat a mistake.
I will — reject greed, or envy other's possessions.
I will — see the need my own happiness to make.

I will — endure with fortitude all life's troubles.
I will — cure them with patient smiles
I will — endeavour to learn from life's lessons
I will — never complain of the numerous trials.

I will — give what I can, in any way I can
I will — live my life to its fullest.
I will — aim to keep healthy my body and mind
I will — disclaim all obstacles as merely a jest.

I will — seek the Lord for help and guidance
I will — for to speak with Him brings comfort to me.
I will — then thank Him for all his blessings
I will — for when you will it, it will be.

Part Five :

ON LIFE AND DEATH

THE BALLAD OF ANNE FRANK

Now I am sitting all alone—on my own
    By the window—no one about,
My mind keeps flitting to the past—through the glass
    Oh dear God please let us out.

How did this happen—wonder why—mustn't cry
    Just sit quietly as a mouse,
Wondering where the earth lies—and the skies
    Nowhere in this tall thin house.

Two long years have gone now—somehow,
    But so many fears that I have known,
I now can share with Peter—sweet are
    All the hours on our own.

If I turn my head outside I see
    Silver raindrops hang on the chestnut tree,
With a sky all blue like a silent sea
    And the gliding gulls with their wings so free.

And I feel a joy when I cast my mind
    To the fields beyond where the rivers wind,
For I know that all who seek will find
    In nature's soul a soul divine.

Friends I am sure will help us—save us
    Life surely could not end this way,
I close my eyes—I'm dancing—prancing
    Surely it will be—if I pray.

But if it happens—that I die—I'll tell why
    In my diary leaf—by leaf,
And when they read it—they will see—some of me
    I'll go on living / after my death.

LIFE AND DEATH

Death I have no fear of thee
So friends shed not your tears for me.
Today I live—so today I'm real,
Tell me now, the way you feel.
Don't keep your praise for when I'm dead
And hurt me now with words unjustly said.
There's a time to live, and a time to die
So I'll not let life just pass me by.
I aim to take each day as a lesson,
Judge my fellow men, not by their purse—
     but by their person
I'll occupy myself with daily giving
And be thankful for the privilege of living.
When at my door knocks trouble and pain,
I'll understand and not complain,
Knowing death brings the ultimate cure,
When life becomes too hard to endure,
For death I view not as an injury,
So when I'm gone—waste not on me your sympathy.

FLOWERS FOR THE LIVING

"He really was such a darling"
You must oft have heard it said.
"I wish he were back among us
I miss him, now he's dead".

Or "if only I could see her again
For I never realised,
How patient and kind she was
Until after she died".

But how useless to sing the praises
Of those who have passed away.
The ones who need it are those
That you meet, day by day.

Just imagine how much it hurts
When you find fault with someone
And criticise their every movement,
But this cannot be undone,

When they have left this world
And their qualities come to mind,
It's to those on this earth
That you need to be kind.

A simple word of thanks
Acknowledgment for a task done well,
Or a few words of encouragement
To those with doubts to dispel.

So when praise and appreciation
You find you feel like giving,
Remember it doesn't help the dead,
Give flowers to the living.

MEMORIES REMAIN

I have tried to drown my thoughts with tears,
    Where Oh where are those long lost years
My heart was filled with sorrow and fears,
    Those memories still remain.

I try to forget but I don't know how,
    How could mankind this thing allow
Though people say you must live for now,
    These memories still remain.

I watched my family die one by one
    The clouds forever now cover the sun,
Friends disappeared, I was left alone
    I cry to the world, Oh what man has done.

I smell the smoke and I hear the cries
    I see the look of wild surprise,
And the fright and terror in the eyes,
    These memories still remain.

47

I have said goodbye to the ones I loved
    And now I ask our God above,
Surely they did not die in vain,
    Help us—that it may not occur again.

For I would forget if I could see
    That man has rejected brutality,
So to open his eyes—make him realize
    These memories must remain.

SEASONS

After a long and weary Winter,
Is it not a wondrous thing
To watch the buds form on the trees
And hear the sweet birds sing,
To feel the warmer air again
And know at last it's Spring.

And from Spring we go to Summer,
When we can enjoy the longer days,
And admire the work of Nature
And see the gardens become ablaze
With the glorious variety of colour
On which we love to gaze.

And then we come to Autumn
When the leaves fall from the trees,
Crisp and brown beneath our feet
And the winds bring a colder breeze,
The birds then take leave of us
And fly across the seas.

And once again it's Winter
With the days dreary and cold,
Everywhere looks so desolate
Weary, sick and old,
Animals disappear and hibernate
Until the better days unfold.

And so it is with mortals,
We have our seasons too,
And when the Winter comes to us
We leave our loved ones to pass through,
To other worlds beyond
And start our life anew.

HOW WILL I BE REMEMBERED

When I look around and see
The wonders of this earth
I ask what good have I done
To justify my birth.

Do I take for granted
Life's precious little gems,
Have I tried to understand
Other people's problems.

Have I stopped to think
About the blessings I've received,
And asked "What can I do
To help others in need".

Have I turned my back
On the troubles of the world,
Or neglected to defend someone
On whom injustice was hurled.

Have I made excuses
For not helping when I can,
Saying "how much can be done
By just one single man".

So when help was needed
Did I then ignore the appeals,
As no snowflake in an avalanche
The responsibility feels.

49

Did I shrug my shoulders
Muttering words of sympathy,
So condoning wrongful deeds
With the sin of apathy.

When finally I close my eyes
And go to meet my maker,
How will I be remembered
As a giver—or a taker.

IN MEMORIAM

To Tom Moule, ND, MB, NOA

Farewell oh true and noble
        spirit
Enriched are we who knew you
And thankful to your everlasting
        soul
That honoured us with a visit.

You've passed but thoughts
        remain
Of help, advice, understanding too
With kindness and knowledge
        No
We'll never see your like
        again.

We, who your good help
        sought
Will miss you, but make promise true
To carry the banner of
        Nature Cure
With the same fervour with which
        you taught.

Part Six :

ON PEACE AND FREEDOM

THE FIGHT FOR PEACE

To sit in a sunfilled garden
With a warm and gentle breeze,
The scent of flowers around you
Birds singing sweetly in the trees.

Or on a wintry evening
What more could one desire,
Than the company of those you love
Sitting peacefully by the fire.

Life certainly would be pleasant
If this way it could always be
But sometimes, it is not,
We have to face reality.

Suddenly, into one's life appears,
Someone who is wickedly bent
On destroying your peace of mind,
On some evil devilment.

Plotting and planning to destroy
Your good and precious name,
Doing evil deeds
And placing on you the blame.

You tell yourself it isn't true
You really don't want to know,
Maybe it will just go away,
But wishing won't make it so.

Then finally you realize
There is only one thing to do,
You must fight back—
You must see it through.

Have faith—find the courage
And though it won't come easily
The Almighty will give you strength
He knows you fight—reluctantly.

For evil is very strong
And ever on the increase,
But Oh, how sad it is!
That the peaceful have to fight for peace.

A LAND RE-BORN

The Jews we are told in the Bible
Wandered for forty long years,
Until Moses found the Promised Land,
And stemmed the people's fears.

For no longer were they Pharaoh's slaves
They'd been freed from his tyranny,
And were once again a nation
Their laws given by God, Blessed Be He.

But the people sinned and disobeyed
And didn't keep the law,
So they were beaten and driven out,
Scattered among the nations once more.

And so it was for generations
They wandered, far and wide,
Always running from persecution
And from tyranny having to hide.

And some forgot their ancestors,
Their religion they did refuse,
For they became assimilated
And denied that they were Jews.

But one day it happened
That another Pharaoh came,
A modern one in Germany
And Hitler was his name.

And he unleashed upon the world
Atrocities beyond belief,
He aimed to annihilate the Jews
And inflicted untold grief.

For six million perished,
Many of whom didn't know
That they descended from Jews,
Until Hitler told them so.

And so after all the horrors
It happened once again,
That the Jews re-claimed their land
For the few that did remain.

They fought hard to obtain it
And in the fighting many fell,
But they won the final battle,
And called the country—Israel.

And though the land is very small
They've opened wide the gate,
For all the Jews who have to run
From persecution, tyranny and hate.

They've worked to till the land
With sweat, toil and tears,
And made the country fertile
Where it was desert for so many years.

And the nation that's emerging
Is free and filled with pride,
Named Sabras—for like the cactus fruit,
They're tough, but sweet inside.

They love the arts and music,
But need an army of defence
For protection from their neighbours,
Whose threats of war are no pretence.

So for this little Haven
Who says "Welcome" to all who come
May it grow from strength to strength
In the national greeting of "Shalom".

TOLERANCE

We live in a world
Where no two people are the same,
And tolerance is a virtue
Which very few can claim.

And we have need of it
Each and every day,
Watching and listening
To what others do or say.

Children who play together,
Men who work side by side,
Shopkeeper and shopper
The range indeed is wide.

Parents to children
And children to parents too,
Each generation is different
And doesn't do what you do.

If we don't have tolerance
In the circle of family life,
Sometimes, not even between
The chosen union of man and wife.

How can we expect tolerance
From the different races on earth
None of whom are responsible
For the destination of their birth?

Because a man is coloured
Or believes in another religion,
Or whose taste in matters are different
And not of your opinion.

That doesn't necessarily mean
That he is wrong and you are right,
And the next thing you know,
Is that you're spoiling for a fight.

The thing that really matters,
It that the code you live by,
Is one that benefits your fellow man,
Or at least you can try.

For how monotonous it would be,
If the same way we all were made,
Where would the beauty in a garden be
If all the flowers were the same shade.

So let us accept that people
Are not all the same,
Some are happy to serve others,
Some seek the hall of fame.

But whichever one you are not
Try to see the other point of view,
For if you show tolerance to them
They'll show tolerance to you.

THE WALL

There it stands, erect and tall
The stones they call "The Wailing Wall".

If stones could talk, what they could tell
Of how the earth becomes a hell,

When all reason leaveth man
And death and destruction is his plan.

What does it mean this piece of wall
To those who stand and loudly call,

To God above to hear their pleas
No more battles—let fighting cease.

This silent wall two thousand years
Has witness death and many tears,

Shed by those who came to pray
For this land—come what may.

But tears and prayers were not enough,
The world says—you must be tough,

For this land you must fight,
Might they say, maketh right.

So they fought three bitter wars
Many lives lost for the cause,

Scattered Jews answered the call
And finally regained the wall.

For Jews this wall—a holy shrine
A symbol that "This land is mine".

A promised land from God above
Rebuilt by labour—a labour of love.

But now let's hope the fighting's done
Though proud we are this wall is won,

Let us pray that wars will cease
That this piece of wall—be the wall of peace.

WAKE UP!

One night as I lay in my bed
   I heard a voice and to me it said.

Wake up from your slumber deep
   What I have to say won't keep,
Are you happy where you are
   Or would you like to travel far,

And see a land—that's small and grand
    That daily grows—and to us shows,

That out of desert green fields are born
    Where once was cactus, now are fields of corn,
Where barren earth gives forth trees
    A land of milk and honey from the bees.

A land that has opened every gate
    To those who run from tyranny and hate,
Where young and old can all find a home
    And are greeted with peace—Shalom.

The people work and do not shirk
    But do their best with zeal and zest,

In a land that's seen so many tears
    But still has hope for the future years,
The scent of orange blossom in the breeze
    A land of milk and honey from the bees.

I woke and said—yes take me there
    I too want to do my share,
They've worked so hard—it must not fail
You must survive—Israel.

LEST WE FORGET THE 1930's

We fought for six long weary years,
A bitter blood-thirsty war,
Against Fascism and Nazism,
Now one begins to ask what for,

Were so many lives sacrificed,
Did they all die in vain?
When we hear the rumblings
Of Fascists and Nazis once again.

Do we not remember
The methods they employed,
The torture, the gas chambers,
The cultures they destroyed?

Are we to be like ostriches
And bury our heads in the sand,
As we did in the thirties
Because we didn't understand,

How much evil would be unleashed,
That every nation came into their plan;
No one was to be exempt
From man's inhumanity to man.

They start with Jews and coloured folk
But the Poles and others soon learned,
That it was only a matter of time
Before they too were to be concerned.

They were dragged off to the labour camps
Or beaten, starved or shot;
We cannot let it happen again
Lest the dead think we forgot.

So we must equip the children
And the full story we should tell,
Of how the Nazis came to power
And brought with them a life of hell.

Prevention is better than cure
Is a saying old but true,
So let us prevent this evil rising
Children, and make a better world for you.

GOOD AND EVIL OR FREE WILL

The world is full of temptations
    Which daily we have to face,
And the choice is our own, in the way we act
    In this modern human rat race.

Do you find a million excuses
    When you're in trouble and transfer the blame,
Are you unjustly angry when things go wrong,
    Wondering from whence the trouble came.

Or are you honest with yourself
    Do you face the cold hard fact,
That you close your eyes to what is wrong
    Because it's so much easier not to act,

And just sit comfortably on a fence
    When there are vital decisions to make;
But if you sit on fences, in time you'll fall
    And the consequences take.

For in this world there's good and evil
    And about the same amount of each,
And the good could combat the evil
    If only we would learn and teach.

That turning a blind eye to injustice
    Is not being tolerant and kind,
But permitting evil to have its way
    Thus, causing heartache to mankind.

If your will is weak, it's no use blaming
    Your neighbour, Parents or friend,
No matter what the influences
    It's your own decision in the end.

For when God created the World
    He provided all—and it was good to see,
But to man he gave free will
    And left the rest to you and me.

WOMEN-WISE

Tired of centuries of wandering
Of being the persecuted few
The Jews were going to Palestine
And in time their numbers grew.

But they came to a barren land
That had very little to give
And to till the soil was essential
To enable them to live.

They came from various countries
With many different ways
Their knowledge very limited
Though their foresight earns our praise.

But those early settlers needed help,
Of every conceivable kind,
Working the land, fighting disease
And even the babies to mind.

So some wise English women
Formed into groups and joined forces,
Giving generously their money and time
Freely pooling their numerous resources.

They opened schools for agriculture.
Teaching hygiene and cooking too,
Creches for babies, homes for children
And gradually *their* numbers grew.

For in many other countries
They organised Women's groups—
Then horror descended upon Europe
Namely Hitler and his Nazi troops.

Then after years of struggle
And a war hard fought and won,
The little land of Israel emerged
And women's work had just begun.

Now their help was needed
Far more than ever before
Providing for the flow of immigrants
Building from shore to shore.

And gradually throughout the world
In towns both large and small
Many women old and young
Have answered the urgent call.

Helping at bazaars and jumbles
And coffee mornings too
Selling tickets, buying some
There's so much for women to do.

For always we must remember
That from the desert, swamp and mire
Hard work has produced Israel
For Jews everywhere "a spare tyre".

Part Seven :

ON ADVERSITY AND ACCEPTANCE

THE UNIVERSITY OF LIFE

To live each day as a lifetime,
            to be aware
            of what each day brings,
To learn from every incident,
            and with fortitude
            bear difficulties,
While enjoying the goodly things.

To listen to a soul in trouble,
            to assist those
            that fall by the way,
Who with your help and compassion
            will regain desire,
            the will to survive,
To face with hope another day.

To have the wit and courage
            To accept and
            conquer adversity,
To admit and learn from errors,
            vowing to repeat them not.
            This is true education,
This, is life's University.

COURAGE

Throughout the world's history
Man's imagination has been fired,
With deeds of great courage
And the men who have it admired.

For with it, men have conquered
And braved fierce enemies,
Climbed the highest mountains
Explored the deepest seas.

But there are other forms of courage
Recognised by very few,
The courage of coping with difficulties
That suddenly descend upon you.

There are those who lose a loved one
On whom they did depend,
Who've lost the meaning of living
And would wish it all to end.

But suddenly they remember
That someone needs them too,
And they still have much to give
So courageously they see it through.

Or those who are sadly stricken
By a vicious or painful disease,
And yet find the courage to smile
And face their sickness with ease.

So while it is most admirable
For man to explore the unknown,
We can show courage daily
And not our misfortunes bemoan.

So when trouble comes your way
And takes you unawares,
Don't give in, just remember
"Courage is fear that's said it's prayers".

FREEDOM FROM WANTING

Thou shalt not covet—the Bible does say,
And most of us think that we don't;
Yet much of our lives are corroded away
By discontentedly crying "I want".

As babies, we're wanting another toy
As children, we just want a lot,
In youth, it's someone else's girl or boy
As adults, what friends and neighbours have got.

This persistent striving and yearning,
For those things we covet and crave,
Shows that we grow without learning
Wanting still—something we cannot have.

Tormenting oneself by constant wantings,
Destroys the ability to measure,
The blessings and joys, daily living brings;
For by seeking pleasure—always we're seeking
pleasure.

By all means be desirous of improvement
Of body, soul, heart and mind,
Then work at it—for nature needs movement;
But that's a requirement of a different kind.

We claim that one's wanting is justified,
"It's for family or friends—not for me",
Then want for them contentment, to be satisfied,
To aim always —from 'wanting' to be free.

I AM AN INSTRUMENT

Our sojourn on this earth is short, and before
this life is spent, in order to be enriched a
mixture of experiences we are sent; and whether
we succeed or fail, we are as it were—
as an Instrument.

64

If the trials are numerous and varied, reject
self-pity and resentment; and when asked by
people who remark, probably with good intent,
"Why you, and why so much?" reply, maybe—
　　　　　because I'm an Instrument.

No doubt you'll have successes too, and be
praised for an achievement, but while accepting
graciously, be not blinded by the compliment;
just remember, knowledge comes for a purpose, via us—
　　　　　as the Instrument.

The key required, is to discard possessions, for
whether good or bad, they're only lent. Even pain,
loss or sorrow is not forever, for nothing is
permanent; accept all things as a learning, be—
　　　　　like an Instrument.

In times of trouble don't indulge in the "Look
what I've gone through" lament; say better
"See what I've *come* through, and much wiser in the
　　　　　event."
for the best lessons are learned from experience, which—
　　　　　requires an Instrument.

The same applies to joys and blessings, be it
wealth, success or environments, these are possessions,
but only on loan, like children are to Parents; so
While loving them, possess them not. Parenthood is—
　　　　　being an Instrument.

And if riding on the crest of a wave, beware
of a sudden descent, to which all are liable,
if we are to be a worthwhile implement; for experience
is wealth and irremovable knowledge. I know, for—
　　　　　I am an Instrument.

COMPENSATIONS

When daily living gets you down,
    And life seems full of irritations,
Of heartaches, problems and sorrows,
    And countless aggravations;
Beware! lest your thoughts lead you
    To feelings of desperation.

Try thinking of those pleasantries,
    That produce a warm sensation,
Think of them morning, noon and night,
    With fervent concentration,
For they're the uplift, the lifeline,
    The rescue from deflation.

It hurts of course when words unkind
    are spoken without hesitation,
Especially when they're thrust at you
    with obvious premeditation;
Particularly, when the truth be known,
    They have no justification.

Where it's possible, try if you can,
    For an honest confrontation,
But if this fails—don't hit back,
    Resist the obvious temptation,
For there's nothing to be gained,
    By spiteful retaliation.

If each of us behaved this way,
    It's surely a fair calculation,
That this example could slowly spread
    Just like a mass demonstration;
Till all men could be brother to brother,
    Then maybe nation to nation?

But to attain such bliss—greet each day
    With hopeful anticipation,
By observing the good things God gave us,
    In his harmonious creation.
Yes! daily extract the best you can,
    There's so much to enjoy—life has its
      compensations.

THE SOWING OF SEEDS

'Tis a pleasure, is it not
       to observe a garden growing;
    The eyes behold its beauty,
    the nose its scent enjoys,
    rewarding is its produce,
But the greatest award of all
      —lies in the sowing.

'Tis difficult of course, at times,
      'specially when limbs are aching;
    To summon the patience,
    to appreciate the merits,
    to plod on—regardless
Of the back breaking efforts
      that go into its making.

'Tis a hard task to be sure
      to be a sower of seeds;
    For flowers, fruit, vegetables,
    or the new born babe,
    all demand much tender care,
While not forgetting, the uprooting
      of destructive weeds.

'Tis wise, when seeds are sown in children
      to give encouragement;
    to firmly, gently tend them.
    Then—as with all seeds
    disturb them not,
But flourish and develop they will,
      with love for nourishment.

'Tis too a pleasure, is it not,
      and precious time's well spent;
    To spread a little happiness,
    to relieve a troubled spirit,
    by showing loving kindness,
By daily sowing seeds—of peace,
      understanding and contentment.

COPING

Life certainly has a habit
Of catching us unaware
And of difficulties and troubles
We all do have our share.

So it's good to be equipped with,
Apart from Faith and Hope,
The will to overcome
And an ability to cope,

A sense of humour helps
Seeing things on the funny side,
And even if the joke's on you
Being able to pocket your pride.

We can't wish away the problems
But let's stop the moans and groans,
And turn the stumbling blocks
Into useful stepping stones.

FRANKIE

Be ashamed, you grumblers
occupied with such trivia,
Look to this indomitable spirit;
Struck down so young,
Confined to bed and wheelchair,
Far wiser and richer you'd be
By paying her a visit.

Not from her the sad talk,
the blames, the criticisms,
The indulgence of self pity;
You'll not find despair,
Reproaches, envy or bitterness,
No signs of regret,
But an air of tranquility.

Here you'll see determination
          You'll witness courage and grit,
But also you will find;
          The body though sadly restricted,
Responds to the warmth of her nature,
          and so much is achieved
Through the clarity of her mind.

Be shamed, you complainers
          of the mundane daily tasks,
and accept them thankfully;
          Take a lesson in understanding,
Wit, endurance and capability.
          Such is the example that is set,
With simple strength—by courageous Frankie.

LESSONS LEARNING AND LIVING

From the moment we waken and open
          our eyes

Till we close them again
          at night,

Life around us is moving
          throbbing,

Things may go wrong or
          they might,

Just alert our minds for decisions
          to make,

And we hope and pray that all
          will come right.

Daily we have numerous and countless
          lessons.

69

And daily we strive and we
yearn

For things to be as we want them
to be,

Unprepared for life's twists—
the turn

That leaves us bewilderd and
wounded

Not aware of the lesson—
the chance to learn.

An experience by itself is so
useless,

If we do not ensure it is
giving

Benefits of understanding and
knowledge

Teaching us when to fight back
or be forgiving.

So in adversity let us not be frustrated
or angry

But take the lesson—learn
and go on living.

THE SEVEN LEAN YEARS

In the Bible we read of seven lean years
And then of seven which are fat,
And all too often life has a habit
Of behaving—just like that.

Things go wrong in quick succession
And no matter how hard one may try,
Even those things which showed great promise
Suddenly switch—and go awry.

Those seven lean years, so dreaded
One's body and soul feel marred,
By constantly coping with troubles
That life appears hopeless—too hard.

But no matter how hard remember always,
That pass the seven years must,
Despair not, the years of plenty are coming,
And while coping, pray—and in the Almighty trust.

TURNING TROUBLES INTO BLESSINGS

I struggled for seven long difficult
                years
Then to their verdict succumbed
                reluctantly.
While the operation was needed, and
                successful,
They cut the pyloric valve, quite
                unnecessarily.

The condition was painful, and hard
                to endure
And relief it appeared was not
                forthcoming.
It confined me to my home—so as is
                my wont,
Decided to turn the trouble, into a
                blessing.

71

Two years it could take they
warned me
Before I would be rid of the
complaint.
So while initially I was shocked
didn't despair,
But called in a teacher, and learned
how to paint.

Thankfully my health now is restored
to me
I've recovered, with added knowledge,
much stronger.
And having put to good use that
trying time
I look not back on those years
with anger.

To those who are suffering, no matter
the reason,
With dragging time that needs
to be killed.
Be wise try a new interest
or hobby,
You'll lessen the burden, and
feel fulfilled.

———————————

Part Eight :

TO "PITTY" MUMMY ON HER 70th BIRTHDAY

Why do I say "to Pitty Mummy?"
That is the first thing I must explain.
You see, I've always thought her very pretty
And I used this endearment to call her name.
When as a young girl I returned from work,
I would call through the letter box
"Hello Pitty Mummy I'm home".
Instead of the customary ring or knocks.

I was always pleased as a little girl
When she had occasion to come to the school,
Proudly thinking, "This is my Mum",
She was different from the accepted rule.
Carrying herself with such dignity,
In appearance clean, pretty and neat,
And though foreign born, spoke beautifully
Had a smiling face, was tactful and discreet.

And even during times of stress—
For in the thirties things were bad,
Her management was second to none,
She always saw to it that we had,
The essential comforts of a Jewish Home.
Candles Friday night, the atmosphere of Shabbos,
Something new to wear, she made each Yom-Tov,
Nothing was too hard when it came to us.

We were known as the three smart girls,
My sisters, Esther, Pauline and I,
For her taste in clothes was exceptional
And her standards extremely high.

73

And even unto this very day,
Though her circumstances are now easy,
Most things she wears, she makes herself
And her hands are constantly busy.

Mummy darling, that we love you
Must be obvious and clear,
So please keep well for our sakes,
For we always need you near,
We wish you a Happy Birthday,
And please God, lots more to come,
In good health and happiness,
Our always lovely "Pitty" Mum.

CHARITY

We have all heard the proverb:
'It's more blessed to give than receive',
But do we understand its meaning
And in its wisdom, believe?

When you think of charity
Is it money only you have in mind,
Or do you know there is charity
Of quite a different kind?

The charity of words,
That can give comfort and peace
To a mind and soul in torment,
And bring them mental release.

That isn't always easy
And often means sacrifice,
But for that particular moment
You've been charitable beyond price.

Of course, we should give money
To those Lady Luck deserts,
According to our means, and generously
Give, until it hurts.

But if you give money
To someone who is in distress,
And then make them feel uncomfortable
They'll be in a bigger mess.

For each of us has to live
With our own individual pride,
And for the giver to hurt it
Makes the receiver want to hide.

Away from his tormentor
Who though generous with his purse,
Is uncharitable with his tongue
And really there's nothing worse.

Or there's the man who is unscrupulous
And earns his wealth ruthlessly,
And then gives large sums of money
In the name of Charity.

Or the woman whose home and family
Are left in the care of others,
Because praise goes more to social workers
Than to conscientious wives and mothers.

There is one thing we should all remember
That Charity begins at home,
And our first duty is to our loved ones
And from this we should not roam.

Do not sacrifice unhappy children
For the glory committee work brings,
First put your home and family in order
And then undertake other things.

So remember we're all in the position
To have the pleasure of giving,
For Charity takes many forms
And puts meaning to the joy of living.

COMMON SENSE

As you journey on life's highway,
To hurdle every fence,
The best thing to be equipped with
Is good, sound common sense.

Of course you'll need loyal friends
And at times, pounds, shillings and pence
But a never failing asset
Is a good supply of common sense.

If only one could give to children
When choosing for them presents
The gift to judge life's situations,
Which is, the blessing of common sense.

There are times when one has problems
Of a size that's so immense,
And there's no one to give advice
Except good old common sense.

So if you don't possess it,
Try from this day hence
To equip yourself for your sake
With good, sound common sense.

HAPPINESS

If you want to be happy
And enjoy this earthly life,
You must learn how to accept things,
Including a certain degree of strife.

Don't look at what your neighbours have
And envy what they possess,
For this will only hinder you
In the pursuit of happiness.

Why not concentrate on giving
Money, time or just your ears
For someone who needs a listener,
They could save a lot of tears.

So much time is wasted
In wanting unobtainable things,
Give, give, with all your might
And you'll see what happiness it brings.

If you must look at others,
Then don't look up, look down
At those whose lot is worse than yours
And would willingly wear your crown.

And even when things go wrong,
Remember it will help to pray
Have faith in The Almighty,
Who'll see you through many a bad day.

For life was not meant to be smooth.
And we all have our turn of sorrow.
It might be your turn today,
But someone else's tomorrow,

Just don't let it get you down
But aim always to be occupied,
Keep your mind and hands busy
You don't know what you can do till you've tried.

And always bear in mind,
That there's no such word as can't
And that happiness is wanting what you have
And not having what you want.

TIME

Time we know waits for no man,
Just you try catching it if you can.
On the other hand it's always there
For you to use—but please, with care.

Some people think time flies away,
Others, that it's been a long day.
How you treat it, it treats you
It all depends on what you do.

If you idle away each hour,
You'll probably feel both bored and sour,
But if you grasp each and every minute
And fill them wisely to their limit,

You will find that time's a friend
From which you can neither borrow or lend.
And time's a wonderful healer—helps you forget
Pain, unhappiness, even sorrow and yet,

It can be against you; for instance when it's said
"I've plenty of time, just one more minute in bed".
You're late for work, you miss the bus
And all day long you're in a fuss.

You can't catch up, and in your ear it drums
"Time that's gone, is gone forever—Tomorrow
            never comes",
It flies so quickly when the right people you're among,
But drags in a crowd in which you don't belong.

For the passage of time is merely relative,
And we should try for as long as we live,
Not to waste it—for that's a crime
But use wisely that precious commodity—Time.

HEAD, HEART AND SOUL

If I could have
  three wishes
And they could all
  come true
These are the things
  that I would wish
My dear children
  for you.

The first wish
  is for the head
To have an open
  uncluttered mind
An ability to see things
  as they are,
Not distorted
  by thoughts unkind.

The second wish
  is most essential
For the times we must think
  with the heart,
When understanding
  and compassion
Help judgment
  to play its part.

And the third wish
  is for the soul
And you ask what that
  might be,
Call it conscience
  call it spirit
Call it eyes
  you cannot see,
But without it
  Man is nothing
An automatic
  mechanical machine

Just going about
      his daily duties
With the beauty around
      him unseen.

For if you lack these
      three essentials
No matter what in life
      you achieve,
You'll be denied
      the ultimate success
The fulfilment of living—
      For I believe
That to communicate
      with our fellow men
Is the greatest achievement
      of all
And to do this
      we need to think
With our Head our Heart
      and our Soul.

I AM A STEERING WHEEL

Like a ship that sails an ocean
      So life seems to be,
Sometimes through calm waters sailing
      Sometimes tossed by the sea,
Often avoiding big deep glaciers
      That only the tips we see;
Holding firmly to the wheel
      While steering to be free.

Or with a hurricane suddenly confronted
      Leaving bruises hard to conceal,
But we still keep on sailing
      No matter how we feel.
For a while, inviting is the horizon
      Ahead appears calm and still;
It's then it's wise to be alert
      Hold steady—I am a steering wheel.

JUDGMENT

There are many do's and don'ts
We learn from childhood on,
Some which we abide by
And some we frown upon.

Those who give advice
Are always pretty sure,
That their particular method
Is the never failing cure.

Of course, it well may be
That for them it's really true,
But what is good for them
May not be good for you.

And also what applies today
May not apply tomorrow,
What brings happiness for some
For others could lead to sorrow.

So we should try to learn
From a very early age,
The benefits of judgment
So that situations we may gauge.

For no matter how much help
Or advice others may give,
It's we ourselves who have to cope
And have our own lives to live.

Of course, we should always listen
To what others have to say,
Listen to various points of view
In order that we may,

See the problem from every angle.
But no matter what we decide,
We can say with confidence
That our own judgment we applied.

81

And should the results be bad
Don't lose heart, but learn,
So that next time you need judgment
You are able to discern,

More clearly between right and wrong
Until gradually you'll be able,
To judge your daily problems
Making like more pleasant and stable.

MAN'S BEST FRIEND

Who looks at you with
    mournful eyes
And lifts her ears in
    mild surprise,
Who seems to feel you've had
    a hard day
And tries to lick your
    cares away.
Who wants to show her love
    is true
By pressing fondly close
    to you,
Who barks when strangers approach
    the door
But for friends bangs her tail
    upon the floor,
Who can't shake hands
    when meeting
But gives her paw in
    friendly greeting,
Who when wanting entry
    scratches on doors
Gently, firmly with long
    lean paws.
When on walks the lead's
    released
Who wags her tail to show
    she's pleased,

Who has become a family
        treasure
Affords us so many hours of
        pleasure,
Who'd sleep on beds if we
        would let her,
Why Rusty! our Irish
        Red Setter
And of her qualities there is
        no end
Our lovely dog, who's
        Man's Best Friend.

MOON MADNESS OR LUNAR-SEA

Marvellous, Magnificent Moon Men—a happening, not a speech,
        They defied the laws of gravity,
        They defied the risks of space,
        Confident that this achievement
        Would enrich the human race.
Yes, now the programme's set—other planets to reach.

They choose for landing the sea of tranquility,
        But so often does man,
        Peace and tranquility disrupt,
        Creating disturbances, disorders
        In turn, making men corrupt,
Yes, and they succeeded—a remarkable technical ability.

But man are you competent such decisions to make,
        Past history has shown us
        How persistently we strain,
        To reach areas unknown
        Speedily grasping for gain,
Yes, we conquer, but not to give—but to take.

Just one magic moment, the World as one became,
          For not just a machine
          Had landed on the moon,
          Earthly barriers had faded
          And there stood—a human.
Yes, but the moment passed—the World is just the same.

Marvellous, Magnificent Moon Men—but is man to man a brother,
          Finds the money and the time
          To conquer the laws of gravity,
          But cannot solve the miseries
          Of War, hunger and poverty.
Yes, Man can reach the moon—but not each other.

THE NEED FOR TRUTH

It's been the pride of mortals, since the time
        of Adam and Eve,

To conquer, to cheat, to outwit, to distort,
        to lie, and to deceive,

The results of which brings forth success,
        we are led to believe.

How readily is man deluded—and so
        'truth to tell', denied,

For it's much more comfortable isn't it,
        a bitter truth to hide,

And more acceptable to believe someone, who has
        oh so sweetly lied.

And how difficult it is to tell the truth,
        knowing it's disbelieved,

For truth's a little something which cannot
        be conceived,

So, in order to be recognised—Truth
    must be perceived.

Then it should be known, and seen and heard
    without a doubt,

For however much lies within, or how good
    the veneer without,

No matter how it's veiled—a lie is a lie; but
    eventually truth will out.

But how is a truth to be recognised,
    repeatedly it's said,

Having listened to both sides, one's usually
    more misled.

True, it's hard to be sure—but if truth were to die,
    The world would be dead.

ODE TO A MOTHER

As I sit reflecting
    Back along the years
I see a mixture of
    Both happiness and tears,
The countless little problems
    Filling life with bother
And with devotion there
    A kind and gentle mother.

Many were the hardships
    The rough and stormy seas,
But we calmly were steered through them
    Seemingly with ease.

85

By an able little lady
    A pleasure to be seen
A friend to all in need, and in
    Her family a Queen.
Always time for others
    Bore everyone in mind
Understood their problems
    No sweeter could you find.

Sometimes there was hunger
    And not too much to wear,
But through you there was always
    Laughter in the air.

Not only what you did, but
    Just your being there,
Gave us so much comfort
    Showing us how much you care.
So willingly and lovingly
    There's nothing we won't do
For your pleasure, for so much
    Dear Mother is owed—to you.

MODERATION

My motto through life has always been,
And it's based on much that I have seen,
If you want the best that life brings
Use moderation please, in all things.

Not too little—not too much
What is needed is just the right touch.
Too many restrictions—too much piety
Brings rebellion among society.

Too few rules and too much rope,
Results in an inability to cope,
Too much play—you reduce the fun,
Too much work and it's never done.

Too much worship of possession
And slowly it becomes an obsession,
No regard for things you own,
And soon you'll develop a heart of stone.

Too many regrets life passes you by,
Too little appraisal you live a lie,
When in trouble don't just rely on prayer
But combine effort with faith—or you'll soon
    despair.

Too many tears you'll be drowned in sorrow,
Too much laughter you'll not heed tomorrow,
So no matter what in life's your station,
To keep a fine balance—you need Moderation.

LEISURE

Leisure—is what we're often craving
    Saying, work is such a chore,
Time—to do just as we please
    For working is such a bore,
What's the use of daily slaving
    What are we working for?
So slowly and surely leisure's increased,
    And now we have time galore.

But what do we, with this leisure
    Do we put it to good use,
Do we happily fill the hours
    Or treat them with abuse?
Does it bring the longed for pleasure
    One expects with time to choose
To develop one's talents and powers
    Or are we mainly on the loose?

Leisure to man is essential of course
But he should know how to use it
Including the time to stand and stare,
To improve his mind, soul and spirit,
To reflect on nature and its source
To develop and learn without limit.
Your leisure is precious, so treat it with care,
As you please—but fill wisely every minute.

VALUES

In this modern world of ours
Are we too bent on seeking pleasure?
Do we in fact exhaust ourselves
In demanding so much leisure?

The working hours get shorter
Which leaves us time to spare,
Do we then put that time to use
Or fritter it away without care?

There are many things we could enjoy
Which in our hurry we pass by,
It's usually the things that go unnoticed
That just beneath us lie.

The company of little children
To watch their minds unfold,
Or listen to the stories
Of someone who is lonely and old.

Or a family get together,
Where no one reigns as king,
But when you can just be yourself,
Relax, converse or sing.

We take so much for granted,
The gifts of sight, sound and speech,
But do we put them to good use
Or seek for other goals to reach?

With our eyes we should try to see
The qualities of our fellow men,
And shut our ears to idle gossip
And speak to praise, and not condemn.

And while thanking God for his blessings,
Let's try and make this vow,
To help those less fortunate than us,
Not sometime in the future—but now!

THE CHILDREN'S VILLAGE

Dedicated to Rabbi and Mrs. Lorenz, and the
Sde Chemed Village and all who reside there.

There is a Rabbi and his wife
    with big and open hearts,
    who once took unto them children,
    some neglected and unwanted
    some just unfortunates,
Victims of a world of strife.

And from just a few came a flow
    of children needing care,
    and then arose the problem
    that obviously they needed
    to be housed—somewhere
For from tiny acorns, oak trees grow.

To sow the seed—precedes the deed
    and something had to be done
    so land was bought with the idea
    that the children should participate—
    learning to create—with love and fun
A large undertaking indeed.

But a seed tended with love and care
    will flourish and increase
    and so it was with the village
    it grew—buildings and children too—
    and from turmoil in their lives, came peace
They learned how to help—how to share.

Knowing that they come from diverse places
    one cannot help but feel pride
    that the example is set by these children,
    that men from different backgrounds
    can live side by side
And the reward—the look of peace on their faces.

GOODBYE SIXTY NINE

Nineteen sixty nine goodbye—soon we'll have to say, and yet
It seems that you arrived only yesterday. But
Now let's look back at the headlines of the year. Needless
Endless fighting, bringing starvation horror and fear, with
Thugs, violence and murder ever on the increase, and
Endangering the lives of those who wish for peace. And why?
Envy and greed seem the motivating force, causing
Nation to fight nation, and all in the name of 'the cause', with

Students discontented, and often rightly so, at the
Injustices meted out, to those we keep so low, as for
eXample the handicapped aged, homeless—oh so many. But
There was of course that incredible moon journey, for the
Year saw the first landing on the peaceful moon, and

Not just machinery, but this time—a human. But oh!
If only our achievements were put to better use, and
Not, as is our wont, each other to abuse. If only we'd
Enjoy, what we take for granted every day
    The flowers, the birds, the winds, the trees that sway,
    The Sun, the Moon, the Stars remain! and are yours and
    mine.
    Remember this—while saying Goodbye to 1969.

MY SISTERS & I

As little girls we three were told
though friends you now are, as you grow old
different paths your lives might take
and destroy your closeness in its wake.

We listened well and we took heed
to prevent this happening, and indeed
it's true, we do live separate lives
for we are devoted mothers and wives.

But the rapport between us is ever strong
through joys and sorrows, right or wrong
we on each other can always depend
for our love and devotion knows no end.

Why this exists is really very clear
whilst showing interest we never interfere
we speak less words that say twice as much
for the understanding we have is such.

That sadly few have ever known
but which we three proudly own
and none can shatter though hard they try
this strong silent bond that runs
                    through my sisters and I.

PRIORITIES

If you're the type that can't say no
are never happier than when on the go
    If you don't know when to stop
    One day you'll just up and flop
If you feel you want all humanity to embrace
It might be necessary this fact to face
    If too long and hard you try
    One day, you will just run dry.

91

While this is jolly good advice
and I sound sanctimoniously wise
    While I know it to be true
    Well—'Don't do what I do'.
While all of the wrongs I tried to right,
Here am I now, with my personal fight
    While all is solved, and peace now reigns
    I am drained,—with aches and pains

Of mankind's problems, there is no end
and those in trouble, know, for whom to send
    Oft times quite unnecessarily
    Without thought, or selfishly
Of course give help, where no one else bothers
Some things though, are more important than others
    Of all activities, there's no need to cease
    But one must get right, the priorities.

SILENT THOUGHTS

Well, here I go again, with yet another
                 lesson to learn
Often have I thought, what the Lord has given
                 I must earn
For somehow, one by one, of each of my senses
                 have I been deprived;
Tanaciously I fought, recouped each one, and
                 thankfully survived.
But one sense was ever dependable and remained
                 good and strong
With it I read talking books, or frequently burst
                 into song.
Now suddenly, I find myself voiceless, or as a
                 concession, whispering,
But with my changed routine, much aware, silently
                 looking and listening.
So while Gods gift of speech, industriously
                 I am now earning
Daily, these are the things that I am
                 observing and learning.

When "Brr-Brr", goes the telephone
                 and I happen to be alone,
There is just nothing I can do
                 except to wonder—oh dear, who?
and when it rings again and again
                 uncomfortably puzzled I must remain.
Oh, what self-control and patience, does that
                 curiosity take.
and what about the phone calls, that I
                 need to make?
Then I switch on the radio—ah listen, a
                 well loved tune
To which, as is my want, I long to accompany
                 with a warbling croon.
But I refuse to be beaten, so while admittedly
                 frustrated I bristle,
Revert I, to a forgotten habit, and defiantly
                 warble and whistle,
And from that same radio, now springs forth
                 all the Worlds news
Words, words, words, many lies, distorted facts
                 and much abuse.
The vengeance, the hate, the hurt, the
                 accusations falsely flung
Oh man, what damage you do with that
                 unleashed, talking tongue.
Come evening, I switch on T.V.
                 to see what there is to see.
Be it fiction or fact, someone's killed
                 that mainly is how the box is filled
and still incessantly, words are flowing
                 where oh where is man going?
But I can't help wondering, how different the
                 World might be
If man was compelled to communicate,
                 without speech, silently.
Would he listen with more care, to a beautiful
                 musical score,
To the countless sweet sounds, he never hears
                 or tends to ignore.
Or would he, if speechless, find other
                 methods to employ

To incite his fellow men, to maim to kill
                    or to destroy
But on second thoughts—Well, it is hard to
                  make up my mind,
For words can soothe too can't they, when they
                are gentle and kind.
I suppose, like in all things, in the end
                man has his choice
as for me, well I'll be jolly glad to get back
                my voice.

WHERE AM I?

Where am I? Who am I?
    I wanted love—you gave me things,
        Oh what sorrow and regret
        Such memories bring.

Where am I? What am I?
    Bewildered—by falseness and pretence,
        Not knowing such unhappiness
        Could result, from tolerance.

Where am I? Sad am I!
    To have lost—those lovely years,
        But I understood your problems
        and quelled your fears.

Where am I? Who am I?
    This—we all have need to know,
        And caring, each for each other,
        Is the way to make it so.

THE MEMORIES THAT LINGER ON

A cherished Mother
Many years passed away
But missed and remembered
Each and every day.
Her tears, her fears
Her lovely smiling face
Precious memories remain
That time cannot erase.

A revered Father
joined her some years after
Leaving impressions of strength
of kindness, of laughter.
His walk, his talk
His special cigarette smoke
He took life in its stride
and enjoyed a good joke.

Beloved Parents
Long since gone—But
We speak of them so often.
That—The Memories Linger On.

WE ARE PEOPLE TOO

Mentally, we wander—lonely as can be
Often bewildered by—what we hear and see
Though fully aware
That our lives are—in some sort of chains
Because, we hear you say—of a lack of brains

Then there are those who—look upon us with pity
Unable to see that—We do have the ability,
Which we can't express,
To realise that we—are utterly defenceless,
When we are needlessly—condemned as useless

And viewing us with—horror or with grief
Is not the way to help—or to bring us relief.
We'd like to explain,
That all of us are—very happy inside
Even, if our disabilities—We are unable to hide

So don't feel pity,—just a little compassion.
Though, of our senses, we—were given short ration,
In our simple way,
We would like to help—others that are in need
For you see, we are not—of a different breed

There's much we could do—if we were taught,
For ourselves, to make things—to learn a little sport?
Of course it needs patience
As we're clumsy when—round about we plod,
But it's not our fault—and we're all children of God

Oh yes, we know there's a sky—and a heaven up above,
And we see all the beauty—of nature that we love.
So try to remember,
That while we're unable—to be the same as you,
We also have feelings—for, We are People too.

ROLES AND RULES

To do or not to do, that is the rule,
The baby, the toddler, the child at school.
Then you're an adult; but they've set your goal,
You're told what's expected, you must fill the role.

Go into your box, don't think,—that's for fools,
Your path has been set, you must obey the rules.
So back you go, into the sheltered hole,
To argue is useless; but it's taken it's toll.

You feel like a puppet, someone else's tool,
Though on the surface, you appear calm and cool.
You know you've been robbed, you're no longer whole;
and you're left, nursing a bruised and battered soul.

YESTERYEARS TEARS

Like the laughing clown
           who hides his frown
Like the song that's sung
           by a heart that's rung
With hurt and numerous pains
Though bravely neither complains.
So well hid are their tormented fears
And the choked, restrained, unshed tears.
Now today you see me weep
And wonder why do I cry
Was it that you were asleep
Or was it that I did lie?
Those years having flown
           I now can own
Often the smile you saw
           was a smile I wore,
While the laughter you heard
Shielded the unkind word.
But having said goodbye
           to those painful years
Today I can cry
           for they're yesteryears tears.

THE NOW

Think not about the years gone by
Forget what's happened, so many say,
But what a waste of past living
If one lives only in the today.

For memory is a gift from God
Which should never be denied,
But whilst remembering, don't forget
The time you laughed, as well as cried.

How sad to have no recollections of
Special occasions, or the face of an old friend
Just as closing the mind to unpleasantries
Means playing the game of "Let's Pretend".

In quelling thoughts of painful times
You risk suppressing joyous ones as well,
So gradually the mind forgets to remember
and you're devoid of experiences—an empty shell.

Remember the fun days, recall the sad
Do so with pride and gratefully
Emerging—one hopes—wiser from the event
and treasuring the wealth of memory.

For each life has it's own memoirs
Usually obtained with the sweated brow
But in remembering the past, look to the future
Which will look back to the memories of The Now.

HOW, WHY AND WHAT

To arrive is one thing
  How you journey is another
To know is one thing
  How you learn is another
To love is one thing
  How you show it is another
To believe is one thing
  Why you're convinced is another
To hunger is one thing
  Why you fast is another
To eat is one thing
  What you digest is another
To talk is one thing
  What you say is another
Do think on these things
  Dear sister and brother.

WE WON'T FORGET TO REMEMBER

In memoriam to a much loved mum.

We won't forget to remember
How you looked in your younger years;
The ready laughter in our home
Mingled often with your tears.

We won't forget to remember
The beautiful things your golden hands made:
The hats, the coats, the dresses we recall,
That from our memories will not fade.

We won't forget to remember
The look of surprise on your lovely face
At the birthday parties we arranged,
No matter the time or the place.

We won't forget to remember
You—at births, barmitzvahs, wedding days.
They'll repeat many times in our memories,
Like a favourite record one plays.

We won't forget to remember
Your warm welcomes, your every little touch.
Forever you'll live in our memory,
For truly we loved you so much.

We won't forget to remember
How at times you'd worry and fuss.
But how calm and peaceful you looked
When finally you left us.

No—we won't forget to remember;
And neither will our families too,
For we've a wealth of incidents to relate,
Helping us to remember you.

A SAD FAREWELL

In memoriam to a much loved dad.

There lies a body set free at last from it's mortal hell
The sufferings gone, the face unlined so who can now tell
That the hard lived years were turbulent up hill and down dell
For with dignity and pride—you withstood them so well.

The hardships you accepted and not morbidly on them did dwell
Whilst bravely you picked yourself up—whenever you fell
You had to succumb finally—as all do, to the Almighty's death
    knell.

But you'll be missed and remembered and time won't break the
    spell.
There's no more sorrow or pain for you no more doubts to
    dispel,
You've earned your rest Daddy darling, we send you a fond
    farewell.

THE LIFE FORCE

Are you in pain or in distress,
is your life on the wain and
in a mess, without a grain of
joy and happiness?
Do you feel sick and constantly
weary, or head so thick and eyes
all bleary, having lost the trick
of being cheery?

Then it's plain to tell you're
ill at ease, in fact it's a spell
which doesn't cease, for your
body's not well, and we call
it disease.
But for every effect there is
a cause, there's been neglect no
time to pause, or even to accept
we've ignored nature's laws.

For the dis-ease we claim is
like a discordant symphony, and no
matter it's name, of which there are
many, we now need to aim to
restore the harmony.
So we must try to achieve to
acknowledge the links, that man's own
web he weaves, in the way he eats
and drinks, breathes and thinks.

But there is help beyond belief,
Albeit of a different kind, from
the air above and earth beneath,
though 'tis hard you'll find whilst
looking for relief, to change
ones habits and mind.
Yet how good it feels when you're
on the right course, and how clearly
it reveals that you're tapping the
source, for in the end only Nature heals
and restores the Life Force.

Part Nine :

IN A NUTSHELL

1. Some people are bad without money—and worse with it.
2. To do the right thing with the wrong people is wasting one's time.
3. The only thing I find intolerable is intolerance.
4. He who is always seeking pleasure—will always be seeking pleasure.
5. You always know the trouble you are in—never the trouble you avoid.
6. He who thinks himself lucky—is unlucky.
7. He who takes—never gets.
8. Communication among people if only we could—for so much is said and so little understood.
9. 'Tis amazing when so little goes into a head, so much comes out of the mouth.
10. What a pity that so many talk so much, and say so little.
11. It's truly amazing how many people live separate lives together.
12. 'Tis such a pity to bury one's head in the clouds—it blots out the sunshine.
13. Waste not the young years—or you'll spend the old ones in tears.
14. Try not to do what you'll regret, for others will remember even if you forget.
15. We can't always teach that which is right—but should try always to prevent that which is wrong.
16. Such is the way of the world—that the peaceful have to fight for peace.
17. How uncharitable is the word charity.
18. The mark of a man's character is not so much what happens in his life—but how he copes with what happens.

19. Would, that man could differentiate between interest and interference.
20. If only man put as much effort into righting a wrong, as he does in denying its existence.
21. How much of life is wasted in those happy only in their yesterdays.
22. Be cautious of the man who thinks he knows it all—the chances are he knows nothing at all.
23. How often people speak the same words—but as though they were a different language.
24. Wish not for the things thou can'st not have—but enjoy to the full the things thou do'st have.
25. Think before *overtaking* on the road, but think before *undertaking* in life.
26. It's not the time you put in—it's what you put into the time.
27. The strength of evil lies only in our own weakness.
28. Avoid the man who raises himself by lowering other men.
29. In living—as in driving—the only justification in looking back, is to ensure the safety of the road ahead.
30. I can forgive him who has wronged me—but can he forgive me for forgiving him?
31. Beware, lest you not be aware, of the difference twixt obstinacy and tenacity of purpose.
32. Look before marriage and overlook afterwards.
33. We are givers all—but some give pleasure and some heartache.
34. Take care lest learning dulls understanding.
35. Confide only in someone with an open mind and a closed mouth.
36. Sometimes what appears to be a set back, can turn out to be a step forward.
37. Does one get the "seven year itch" because things have not been up to scratch!
38. If you want to get something off your back—turn round and face it.
39. Nothing is mine, yet everything is mine—that is—mine to care for, to tend, therefore I am the keeper of, what is his.
40. Be wise and recognise the claim "I do not demand", for they do expect and it has the same effect.

Part Ten :

YOUR HEALTH IN YOUR HANDS

In July 1969 the Author, Bertha Klug underwent major surgery, which resulted in a severe digestive problem, which in turn led to other complications.

In gratitude for her recovery in March 1977, she founded a Clinic (with nominal fees) for Natural Therapies. The "Wessex Healthy Living Foundation" is a non commercial, non profit making Registered Charity, Motto "YOUR HEALTH IN YOUR HANDS". 72 BELLE VUE ROAD, SOUTHBOURNE, BOURNEMOUTH BH6 3DX.

Further information, as follows:-

TO HELL AND BACK

In July, 1969, I underwent major surgery for the repair of a hiatus hernia. The operation, which was performed in one of London's most reputable teaching hospitals, was apparently very successful, but the surgeon performed at the same time—and, I have since been told, quite unnecessarily—a pyloroplasty, which means cutting the pyloric valve which controls the passage of food from the stomach into the intestines.

For four days after the operation I was allowed to have no food or drink, but was kept on a "drip" (which means being fed intravenously). For the following three days I was given liquids only, and on the eighth day—when, in the opinion of the medical staff, I was making a wonderful recovery—I was told quite emphatically by the surgeon that I should now eat normally. In other words, I was to have three three-course meals daily, plus a good tea, to "rebuild my strength". My initial reaction was one of disbelief that my stomach would be able to cope with "normal" feeding, particularly as it had not been accustomed to doing so during the past seven years, because of the hiatus hernia. Hitherto, in order to keep relatively fit and active, I had been compelled to eat "little and often". However, those were the surgeon's instructions to the sister and staff, and I, the patient, had *no say whatsoever*.

Nearly Choked
On the 10th day after the operation I very nearly choked during the lunch-time meal, and that was the start of what from then on were referred to as "the attacks". The symptoms ranged from severe, spasmodic pains across the chest and heart to an internal "battle" in the stomach leading to extreme nausea, pouring perspiration, violent hiccups, a general withdrawal of strength and sometimes even a state bordering on coma.

It was quite obvious that something was very seriously wrong. I observed—it was difficult not to—that all "the attacks" were associated directly with meals and that, far from "building my strength", any strength I had was drained from me after eating or drinking. The length and severity of the attacks were clearly related to the amount of food I had consumed, and it was obvious to me that I

105

was only able to eat very small quantities, and that I required them frequently.

I pleaded with the surgeon and explained that my stomach was pleading with me to be treated gently, but help was not forthcoming from that quarter, for if a professional man will not admit to the existence of a condition, he cannot even begin to consider how to deal with it. Consequently, I was subjected to various tests, each of which revealed nothing, although while I was enduring the tests, the attacks increased in severity.

Bewilderment

There was a general air of bewilderment about the surgeon and also throughout the staff, and I was even told by the registrar that I had "very odd symptoms indeed". Because of these opinions, I was beginning to think that I was some sort of a freak.

On my insistence, after nearly three weeks of much suffering—though, believe it or not, I was a bright, cheerful patient and quite energetic between meals—a stomach specialist was called in, and he diagnosed immediately a "classic" case of what is called "dumping Syndrome" which leads to a state of hypoglycaemia, in which there is a low level of sugar in the blood, associated with hyperinsulinism—an excess of insulin (the opposite of diabetes). All this, apparently, had been caused by the surgeon cutting the pyloric valve.

The condition was one which would not be revealed by the X-ray examination or the tests to which I had been subjected, but only by the evidence that nature provides, i.e. the general condition of the patient. It was now quite obvious why the surgeon had disputed my private doctor's suggested diagnosis of dumping syndrome when the attacks first started, as it would appear to be a reflection on his work.

Most Concerned

The best advice that the stomach specialist could give me—and he was most concerned about the condition and extremely kind to me—was that I should eat little and often, almost hourly, have no carbohydrates or animal fats, but to take massive amounts of protein, mainly in the form of lean meat and fish; eggs, cheese and milk were ruled out, because they brought on the attacks. All food, liquid or solid, was to be taken preferably lying in bed and leaning to the left, or in a reclining position in an armchair with my feet up. All this was necessary to compensate for the defective pyloric valve. The alternative? An operation to repair the valve!

In the opinion of the specialist it was an "appalling condition to endure", because the attacks, once they started, lasted from 1 to $1\frac{1}{2}$

hours. The complete cycle was as follows: Within about five minutes of eating there was an increase in body heat and a distended and rumbling stomach, coupled with a general feeling of weariness, extreme nausea, leading to retching and sometimes vomiting. This was followed by what I can only describe as uncontrollable reflex belching or hiccups, cold perspiration pouring from the body from head to toe, a general feeling that life was receding from the body, the blood drained from the face and even the fingers, severe pounding in the heart, sometimes accompanied by spasm pains across the chest and heart. As the attack neared its end, a kind of phlegm was regurgitated from the stomach to the mouth, and not until this discontinued was the attack over.

Terrible Weariness

When the blood-pressure was taken during an attack it had dropped to 80. But, oh, the relief when the attacks subsided—although they left in their wake a terrible weariness.

I was discharged from hospital and kept strictly to the method of feeding that had been advised by the specialist who also prescribed various drugs. Three months passed, and so very nearly did I, for, while I was able to ward off many of the severest "dumpings", not a day passed without at least one attack, even the smallest of which drained me completely. My "life-line" to sanity during this hour and a half of hell was a game of *Scrabble* with one of the children.

Added to all this, the drugs—as is their wont—were inflicting side-effects, while doing very little to alleviate the "dumpings".

By the middle of October, I was beginning to wonder whether I would ever be rid of this condition. The thought of further surgery was abhorrent to me, and I was at a loss to know where else to turn for help. It was then that a very dear friend advised me to consult a naturopath, and from here on my story is of a totally different "nature"—if readers will forgive the pun!

From the beginning, the practitioner I consulted understood the condition, he explained in detail what my digestive system was having to endure and how nature cure would enable my body to heal itself. Provided I followed his instructions, did not deviate from the diet, and paid heed to the signals which nature constantly provides.

When I first went to him, my blood-pressure was 90/60, and I was suffering from all that that entails, plus numerous discomforts, pains and general debility. He immediately put me on to a rigorous, finely measured, well balanced diet, consisting mainly of salads, fruit and lightly cooked vegetables, fruit and vegetable juices, and a little poultry, lean meat and fish. Above all, he suggested substitutes from the health stores for the animal fats which I was unable to digest, but which the body requires, and which it had been lacking for the past three months. He also gave me some special osteopathic treatment designed to release spinal tension and improve the circulation and nerve supply throughout the body. While I was having this treatment, I experienced one or two "healing crises" which have been treated by fasting, followed by the prescribed diet. The results would have astonished anyone who thinks he will starve if he misses a meal!

Healing Crises
For the benefit of newcomers to nature cure, a "healing crises" usually occurs when the condition is improving. As vitality begins to return, the body, as it were, reproduces the symptoms of the condition under treatment, and frequently also of past illnesses which have been suppressed by drugs. To help the body to cope with the "crises", it is advisable to rest the digestive organs and to fast. My own condition would not permit complete fasting, and so I was allowed to have fruit-juice drinks every few hours for as many days as the practitioner deemed necessary.

After the fast, there was a gradual return to feeding by introducing liquid foods such as *Bio-Balm* and *Emprote* once or twice daily, for a few days, then one salad meal for a few more days, working slowly back to normal, healthful feeding. It is as well to emphasize that these crises, followed by the fasting—unlike the effects of medicine or drugs—do not merely reduce the symptoms, but effectively rid the body of the *causes* of illness.

In fairness to the surgeon, I must say that the hiatus hernia operation was a success. For seven years, from the time the hiatus hernia had revealed itself, life had been extremely difficult, because I was subject to recurring attacks of bronchial pneumonia throughout the winter, which meant that, from October to March, I kept going on antibiotics which, in turn brought side-effects and problems. But while I am very grateful to the surgeon for having performed a successful repair, I am still puzzled as to why he cut the pyloric valve, and am appalled at his lack of understanding when things went wrong. The closest he came to an apology, after the final diagnosis, was, "Well, you know that life is trial and error," to which I replied, half jestingly, "Thank you—my trial, your error." Believe me, it was no joke, but keeping one's sense of humour was the only way to maintain a sense of balance and keep from breaking down.

At the time of writing, some 18 months after the operation, I have not had a "dumping" for many weeks. Nature soon lets me know if I tend to abuse her diet-wise. My blood-pressure has risen to 122/76, and my vitality and zest for living have returned. I have not taken a drug of any kind since starting nature cure treatment.

I have occasional slight adjustments to my diet according to progress, although it is still necessary for me to eat small, frequent meals, and to avoid mixing liquids with solids. Joy of joys, I can now eat normally at the table, provided that I remain seated for 15 minutes or so afterwards.

While this whole episode in my life has been, to say the least, a painful and severe experience for me and my husband and four children—it had, in fact, completely disrupted our family life—I feel, now, that I have learned so much that I am almost glad to have gone through it all, for I am emerging much wiser.

Yes, it's been a hard road, but a worth-while journey, and I only wish that more people—including the medical profession—would learn to listen to Nature. She holds the key to health.

I reached my half-century this year, and now feel that life can begin at 50.

SO—WHAT'S A HEALING CRISIS?

It is now two years since I started living the nature cure way. The reason I did so is, I suspect, the same as that which would be given by most devotees to nature cure. It is ironical, is it not, that one usually comes round to the *natural* way of living via the *unnatural* way—having run the gamut of orthodox methods, drugs, etc., which have failed.

The details of the chain of events which led me to nature cure were published in the February 1971 issue of HEALTH FOR ALL in an article entitled "To Hell and Back", but for the benefit of new readers, following an operation for hiatus hernia I was left with a condition called "Dumping syndrome", accompanied by hypoglycaemia.

For three torturous months I was subjected to violent upsets, following the intake of food or drink. All the doctors' advice and medicines gave no more than temporary relief, but they also produced various side effects, which in turn created further problems.

So, it was a case of "When all else fails, what can you lose?", and like many other converts, it was in this desperate frame of mind that I turned to nature cure when a friend suggested that I should try unorthodox treatment.

Confident
The naturopath whom I consulted was very sympathetic and understanding. He was also confident that the condition could be cured, and that my depleted strength would return, provided that I adhered to the nature cure methods which, he explained, would remove the obstacles which prevent nature from functioning properly in healing bodily disorders. Most of our health problems, he explained, are brought upon ourselves, by our abuse of nature in the way we eat and conduct our lives generally.

He warned me to expect something which he termed "a healing crisis", and explained that by discarding all suppressive drugs, and by eating mainly raw, uncooked fruit and vegetables—which have an eliminative effect—nature "throws up", as it were, all those symptoms which have been suppressed by drugs, or which have become bogged down by faulty feeding.

The term "healing crisis" was completely new to me, and yet, when

110

the principle was explained to me it made much sense, under the premise that what goes in, must come out. Anyway, I was by this time prepared to undergo any treatment which would rid me of my burden of ill health and restore my vitality.

The practitioner also warned me that any past illness or symptom which had been suppressed by antibiotics or any kind of suppressive treatment, would probably come to the surface, and be revealed in terms of a healing crisis. As I had been subjected to quite a number of suppressive treatments—for a variety of reasons, too numerous to mention—I knew that if the nature cure theory was correct, I could expect to undergo some very drastic healing crises.

From the day of my first consultation I discarded all drugs, pills and artificial aids of any kind, and threw myself completely into the nature cure way of living.

Ideally, the naturopath would have preferred to start me on a fast straight away, but owing to my weakened condition, and its nature—which required me to eat little and often—this was not possible immediately. However, within a very short time—when I was feeling considerably stronger, and the "attacks" had become milder and less frequent—I awoke one morning to what were obviously the signs of my first healing crisis, confirmed later in the day by the naturopath.

Different
Most of those around me—admittedly well-meaning and concerned for my welfare—could see only that I was ill, and I certainly felt ill, and yet . . . and yet, it was a *different* feeling, although one could not dismiss the fact that the effects still had to be dealt with.

It was then that the naturopath decided that the time had arrived when I should undergo *my* first fast. It lasted for eight days, during which time I was allowed nothing but specially selected fruit or vegetable juices a few times a day, for, as I have already explained, my particular complaint did not permit complete fasting.

On the first day I was a little hungry, on the second I was a little sleepy, and on the third day a little weary, but on the fourth day the symptoms of the condition were obviously clearing, and I was beginning to feel stronger. At the end of the eighth day I felt that I could have continued to fast indefinitely and my vitality, both physical and mental, had returned. Without drugs or artificial aids of any kind, all the symptoms of the healing crisis had disappeared and I felt *cleansed*.

That healing crisis was the forerunner of many others which I have experienced during the past two years, each of which has been treated by fasting for periods varying from three to ten days, according to the severity and nature of the symptoms.

Welcomed
What I should like to emphasize to anyone who contemplates embarking on a course of nature cure treatment, is the inestimable value of a healing crisis. As I stated at the beginning of this article, I have experienced in my life a variety of—for want of a better word—illness, or conditions, brought on after prescribed medication, each of which has reappeared during the past two years. I have welcomed them, dealt with them—mainly by fasting—and each time I have felt more cleansed by the process.

The nature cure theory of the healing crisis, and curing by fasting, is based on the fact that drugs do not *cure* illness but merely mask and suppress the symptoms, thus causing unpleasant side effects, and quite frequently giving rise to other conditions, as I know only too well! In fact, "illness" is regarded as nothing more than a breakdown in the body's natural curative processes, caused mainly by incorrect feeding and excessive medication.

Having lived in the orthodox way for the major part of my life—nearly 50 years—and only for the last two years according to the so-called unorthodox or nature cure way, I can vouch for the effects of both ways of living.

"Side Effects"
I am reminded, here, of the times I have said to various medical men—who were plying me with medication for an undiagnosed condition, and dismissing the reactions I was describing as "merely side effects"—"You seem to be unaware that these so called 'side effects' are not something apart from the body, but are occuring *inside*, thus giving the body more problems to cope with, and it seems to me that one needs to be very healthy in order to survive an illness and its treatment!"

I recall, too, the times when, during the course of medical treatment, I felt thoroughly depleted and lacking in the vital force which I knew I should possess—and which I felt was being suppressed. I was told by various doctors that "as one gets older, one must expect a decrease in energy".

Now, I would like to ask these same men what explanation they can give for the fact that, years later, I feel so many years younger. My almost limitless vitality and varied activities—in addition to my ordinary domestic duties as a wife and the mother of four children—provide irrefutable proof of this.

After two years, the healing crises are now rare, and they are very mild when they do occur. I know exactly how to deal with them, nature itself being my first guide. They no longer interfere with daily living, and I also find that a voluntary, weekly, 24 hour fast—on liquids only—is very beneficial.

This too does not restrict me in any way.

Eternally Grateful
My naturopath—to whom I am eternally grateful—tells me that when the body has rid itself of the accumulation of suppressive drugs the healing crises will cease altogether. As everything else that he explained to me, with regard to nature cure and healing crises, has been borne out by personal experience, I have every reason to believe that this prediction too, will in the course of time prove to be correct.

To all readers who are experiencing their first healing crisis, and who may be tempted to give up, particularly when pressurized by well-meaning family and friends, I say "*Don't* give up, but persevere, and learn for yourself the value of these healing crises." If the term "healing crisis" sounds dramatic, and is unnerving, think of it more in the nature of a *healing reaction*, which is what it really is.

In conclusion, I can only say that it has been an amazing experience to be confronted with old, suppressed conditions, both physical and emotional—for they are inevitably connected—to face them, discard them without artificial aids of any kind, and to feel rejuvenated afterwards.

Charity No. 274208

WESSEX HEALTHY LIVING FOUNDATION

under medical supervision

72 BELLE VUE ROAD,
SOUTHBOURNE,
BOURNEMOUTH, BH6 3DX
TEL: 0202 422087

What is the . . .

WESSEX HEALTHY LIVING FOUNDATION?

It is a non-profit making registered charity charging nominal fees to the public. Membership entitles further benefits.

CLINIC

Homoeopathy, Osteopathy, Naturopathy, Physiotherapy, Acupressure, Acupuncture, Aromatherapy, Dietetics, Reflexology. Herbalism, Chiropractic, Hearing Specialist, Massage, Hypnotherapy, Counselling.

EDUCATION

Lectures, courses, group therapy, meditation, health topics, vegetarian cookery.

INFORMATION

Practitioners, health resorts, where to shop where to eat, where to stay, training courses.

Open Monday – Friday 9.00 a.m. – 5.30 p.m.   Saturday 9.00 a.m. – 2.00 p.m.

AIMS AND OBJECTS

Recently there has been a greater awareness by people of all ages of the importance of natural therapies. Perhaps this has come about as a reaction against the artificial life style, environment and diet of the 20th century. This has been brought to the attention of the public by the media. Unfortunately the information and educational facilities available to the public is frequently inadequate and expensive. The various therapies that come under the umbrella of natural therapeutics are beyond the purse of those within the lower income groups the aged and unemployed, as most of the natural therapies are not included in the National Health Service.

The Wessex Healthy Living Foundation Centre has been open to the public since March 1977, making Bournemouth the FIRST TOWN in the country to have its own Natural Therapeutic Day Centre. Being a registered charity enables us to give over one hundred consultations and treatments each week by qualified voluntary dedicated practitioners in the field of Holistic Medicine—to people who would otherwise be deprived of this choice. A wide variety of therapies UNDER ONE ROOF.

We receive and reply daily to enquiries by letter and telephone from all over the British Isles (and overseas) seeking assistance or advice for their personal and health problems, or for opening centres such as ours in their own towns. Education Classes, Lectures, Public Meetings and Speakers for other societies are arranged, all for the purpose of achieving and maintaining good health. Our monthly Education Meetings, talks and demonstrations are well attended giving the public an opportunity at 'Question Time'.

We offer to the young a programme of prevention, and to those in middle years and the elderly an opportunity to maintain a better quality of life, and to cope more easily with the stresses of modern living, i.e. anxiety, headaches, tiredness, depression, constipation, problems of overweight, excessive smoking, drinking and numerous other more serious conditions, at very low fees.

The Trustees and Management wish as many people as possible to benefit from the use of the Centre. There is a 25% reduction on clinic fees to members and a reduction to any of the lectures and demonstrations, on production of membership card. There are many other benefits—see Membership Form and other Literature at the W.H.L.F. Centre.

To alleviate the pressure at the W.H.L.F. a Clinic the BOURNEMOUTH NATURAL HEALTH GROUP PRACTICE was opened in January 1981.

UNDER ONE ROOF . . .

CHERYL ISAACSON REPORTS ON AN ALTERNATIVE CENTRE WHERE THE PRACTITIONERS WORK FOR FREE, SO THAT FEES ARE KEPT LOW.

A comfortable house on the outskirts of Bournemouth is the unlikely setting for a new concept in natural health care. A homeopath, naturopath and osteopath and other alternative practitioners have got together to form a clinic. Without any "mine's the best" conflict they provide a complete range of therapies for the 100 or so patients booking every week.

Holistic medicine is their aim. And what is more they give their services free.

The Wessex Healthy Living Foundation is a registered charity under the chairmanship of tireless campaigner for the spread of natural therapy Bee Klug. It got off to a shaky start in March 1977, wobbled to its feet with morning sessions only and is now a going concern six days a week.

Not only a clinic, more a way of life is a reasonable description as patients, who come from far and wide, get involved not only in their own treatment but also in lectures, discussions and events leading to a totally new approach to health.

Bee Klug doesn't like to talk about "alternative" medicine or nature "cure". She believes firmly that the Wessex Healthy Living Foundation must work with the medical knowledge already around and give hope not with dramatic effect but the realisation that "your health is in your hands".

It wasn't a simple idea to put into practice. Stresses and strains beset its inception but Bee feels the story is of a "nightmare that became a dream that became a reality". She is breathing more easily now the clinic has reached a consolidation period building up a busy list of therapies that's a joy to her eyes.

A first-time patient usually consults the homoeopathic doctor—also qualified in orthodox medicine—for a broad general view. Then he may recommend other specialists at the clinic for further visits. Tensions may be worked on by the masseur, who might then discover a lesion better dealt with by the osteopath.

The half-hour's initial consultation often surprises those used to being rushed in and out of a doctor's surgery. It gives ample time for the one thing considered vital in the Foundation: talking out your problems. They believe many ills often result from pent-up emotions and mental "states", and are eased simply by getting to the underlying tensions. A special counsellor is available to give gentle encouragement to "let go" without hypnosis, group encounters or anything that might frighten off the first-time patient.

All the practitioners are heavily booked, often three months in advance, with reflexology and aromatherapy as special favourites. The osteopath and chiropractor are also much in demand.

One of the principles Bee felt most strongly about from the start was that the clinic should not be a commercial venture. Practitioners were to work there on a voluntary basis. "It'll never work", she was warned by pessimists who assured her this was the way to get the worst practitioners . . . ones who would virtually pay her to get patients. But Bee went ahead and asked each one she wanted for half a day of dedication a week and it worked. All the practitioners are well qualified and come from colleges of repute. The manager, Ernest Winterbottom, and two receptionists are the only paid staff.

Bee thinks therapists want to work at the clinic because of two unique factors. One is that they can interact with each other. At regular meetings each lets the others know exactly how their therapy works and the kind of results they have been getting. That way they can get outside their own speciality and see it in the context of literally holistic medicine.

They also appreciate treating patients they would not ordinarily see: people tentatively entering the field of alternatives rather than the converted. For new patients, becoming interested in what's happening inside after years of taking what the doctor ordered can present strange problems. If they take on the task of looking at what's going on in their own bodies they are afraid they will become hypochondriacs. So they have to be shown that it just means being aware, not thinking too much about it.

Nevertheless the clinic's clientele has grown in a way that's been rewarding for Bee. At first, she recalls, it was a bit like a mothers' meeting and though she was happy to help the middle-aged ladies, the major aim was to "get it across to everyone". Now men, children and young mothers all drop in, she notes with satisfaction.

Fees are kept to a minimum—prices most people can afford.

Though Bee would not like it said, a major influence on the steady influx of practitioners and patients must be that she is behind it. She is a person of exceptional energy and ability. A wife, mother-of-four, window dresser turned interior designer and—in her spare time— semi-professional actress. She is also the kind of visionary who makes things work when all around her are saying, "No, it couldn't possibly".

Her vision of the Wessex Healthy Living Foundation followed a conversion to natural therapies which is one of those true "sudden enlightenment" stories.

Some 12 years ago she was a very sick woman. A successful operation for a hiatus hernia also entailed cutting the pyloric valve, which controls the passage of food from the stomach into the intestine. The result of this admitted surgical error was attacks that even her specialist called "appalling".

While she was suffering she felt strongly that she was being guided towards something. When a friend recommended a naturopath Bee suddenly knew she was on the right path. Her exhausted body responded quickly to fasting and a wholefood diet and she had her first experience of the "healing crisis"—though she prefers the term "healing reaction".

She wasn't cured but she did get a lot better. She also learned to be careful and what she could do to help herself. Natural therapy rang bells deep within her because it echoed the kind of common sense she had been brought up on: "sweating out" childhood illnesses and the importance of "keeping the bowels open".

Going back to these principles was, she recognised, the only way to real health. She came out of the despair of illness knowing she must "dedicate the rest of my life to putting natural therapy on the map".

The idea wasn't new to Bournemouth. Interested parties had been making noises about founding a clinic devoted to alternative medicine for some time; holding meetings that ended in discord because nobody could agree on what form it should take. Some factions wanted just one therapy. Others were for a mixture of everything that could be gathered under the alternative umbrella, making it a mind/body/spirit cornucopia of palm-reading, faith healing, radionics, right out to the farthest fringes.

The clash of personalities ended when Bee took over and set up a management council composed of herself, a homoeopathic doctor and an osteopath and naturopath. They all agreed on drawing the line at anything "way-out". They were adamant about not frightening people off before they had a chance to appreciate the whole new way of thinking the alternative system demands.

Bee is quick to point out that this in no way reflects personal opinion. For her, anything that makes people healthier and happier is worth a try. But gently did it at first with no "strange goings-on behind closed curtains". Above all the clinic had to be acceptable to the majority for whom "alternative" meant "suspect".

There was a time when Bee wondered if she was setting-up a natural therapy clinic because people ought to want it . . . or was there a real need? But if she questioned her motives then she has no need to do so now.

People whose doctors never let them know what was really wrong with them, who were palmed off with painkillers. People who felt guilty about wasting surgery time whenever they needed reassurance. And people whose health problems seemed to go round in ever increasing negative circles. For them and all who want to get away from the feeling that "they" are only interested if you are getting worse, the Wessex Healthy Living Foundation is offering positive counteractive measures.

They offer the treatment of the individual as a whole, instead of isolated physical parts. A choice of therapies that work steadily and gently, without side-effects. Caring advice, with time to talk over your condition. But above all the holistic approach to health everybody needs.

A NATURAL WAY OF LIFE

(Edited) by Elizabeth Edwards

Dorset Life March 1974
Practitioners of fringe medicine, homoeopathy, acupuncture and the like, at one time were considered as types of 'Quacks' and the people who followed these methods were considered 'cranky' and even a little 'odd'. All this changed some time ago; respectability has been achieved, aided by the grateful thanks received from the many sufferers who found healing where before there seemed to be only pain and discomfort.

Quite recently both our present Queen and Prince Charles, have spoken out in public about their beliefs in natural medicine and its healing qualities. Other members of the royal family, including the Queen Mother, Princess Margaret and the Duke of Gloucester all favour alternative medicines.

The seal of royal approval has popularised treatments formerly regarded suspiciously by some people. This has been particularly encouraging to the founders of the Wessex Healthy Living Foundation in Belle Vue Road, Southbourne, Bournemouth, who's motto is "Your Health in Your Hands". There, a list can be studied of devoted and skilled practitioners who give their services free to the Foundation. This enables those with low incomes to receive treatments, formerly out of their financial reach, for a nominal sum.

Bournemouth is fortunate in having the services of the Healthy Living Foundation. But how did this marvellous organisation come about? To start at the beginning—the Foundation owes its inception to the determination and dedication of Mrs. Bertha Klug, a lively and well known Bournemouth personality.

In 1970, after seven years of pain and suffering from digestive problems she underwent a serious operation for hiatus hernia when her pyloric valve was also cut in error, resulting in prolonged periods of acute discomfort when it was virtually impossible to eat anything; all attempted meals were followed by long periods of nausea, weariness and pain, the traumatic suffering lasting for up to one and a half hours. The condition seemed as though it would continue indefinitely and life became a series of nightmares until a dear friend advised her to try naturopathy.

The results of this treatment, based on diet (she became a Vegetarian and is a Life Member of the J.V.S.), massage and an understanding practitioner were so successful that 'Bee', as she is known to her many friends, decided to devote the remainder of her life to helping others to regain their lost health. In her own words "I vowed to the Almighty that when I recovered I would somehow be instrumental in setting up a Natural Health Day Centre incorporating all the therapies under one roof".

In conjunction with Medical Adviser, Dr. Harling, a homoeopathic physician the Wessex Healthy Living Foundation was established on St. Valentine's Day, February 14th, 1977. The Foundation opened with four voluntary Practitioners, no patients and no members. Today there are 24 Practitioners who deal with over 100 patients each week and approximately 2,000 members.

The main beliefs of the Foundation (which is a registered charity) are that prevention is better than cure and to make available therapies to the public at a price they can afford through education, information and attendance at a clinic of qualified, natural therapeutic practitioners.

Organising the non-profit making project, finding and equipping suitable accomodation, obtaining charity status and raising the necessary funds to start the venture took dedication, hard work, flexibility, patience, prayer and even a sense of humour when difficulties seemed insurmountable.

By opening the Centre, Bournemouth became the first town in the country to provide a wide variety of natural therapeutic treatments, with nominal charges, and under one roof.

It has to be stressed that the Wessex Healthy Living Foundation is not against the orthodox medical profession, rather it co-operates with it. As Bee again says, "Some of my best friends are doctors. We feel that people should be given freedom of choice and hopefully one day, we will not talk of alternative therapies, but complementary ones, as much can be done to relieve overworked doctors.

When Bee stressed to enquirers that the clinic was not a commercial, profit-making venture and that both the Administrator and the Practitioners were to work on a voluntary basis, much criticism was received from well-intentioned persons who warned her that in this way she would not get the best type of practitioners. But Bee went ahead and it worked! All the practitioners are well qualified, were trained in colleges of repute, and are dedicated.

Bee feels that one of the advantages of the system is the interaction of the practitioners. Through discussions and meetings they are made aware of the best treatments for patients.

The wide range of therapies include massage, osteopathy, aroma-therapy, reflexology, acupuncture, acupressure, chiropractice, hypno-therapy and constructive advice from a social counsellor.

121

The Wessex Healthy Living Foundation advocates the treatment of the individual as a whole and not in isolated physical parts. It offers a choice of therapies that work steadily and gently without side effects, caring advice and above all, a holistic approach to health problems. It stands for a positive way of life and helps to develop the right mental attitude together with harmony of mind and body.

The success of the Wessex Healthy Living Foundation is mainly due to the dedication, hard work and enthusiasm of the Chairman and Hon. Administrator Bee Klug, Vice-Chairman and Hon. Secretary Pauline Sumeray, Hon. Treasurer Joel Levene, the Manager Ernest Winterbottom and other supporters. The success and gratitude of many patients have made the difficulties of early days seem more than worthwhile.

Happy smiles after the 7th Progress Meeting of the Wessex Healthy Living Foundation. From L to R. Alderman Harry Mears, Dr. Harling, the Mayor and Mayoress of Swanage, Mrs. Bertha Klug (Chairman) Ernest Winterbottom (Manager), Mr. Eric Morgan (Patron), Mrs. P. Sumeray (Trustee), Mr. Klug, Mrs. Doris Grant (Patron).